THE WAY
THEY PLAY

THE ACOUSTIC ROCK MASTERS

by HP Newquist and Rich Maloof

D1285790

Backbeat Books

San Francisco

Published by Backbeat Books
600 Harrison Street, San Francisco, CA 94107
www.backbeatbooks.com
email: books@musicplayer.com
An imprint of the Music Player Group
Publishers of *Guitar Player*, *Bass Player*, *Keyboard*, and other magazines
United Entertainment Media, Inc.
A CMP Information company

CMP
United Business Media

Distributed to the book trade in the US and Canada by
Publishers Group West, 1700 Fourth Street, Berkeley, CA 94710

Distributed to the music trade in the US and Canada by
Hal Leonard Publishing, P.O. Box 13819, Milwaukee, WI 53213

Cover and text design: Richard Leeds - bigwigdesign.com
Cover photo: Kelly A. Swift / RETNA

Library of Congress Cataloging-in-Publication Data

Newquist, H.P. (Harvey P.)
    The acoustic-rock masters / by HP Newquist and Rich Maloof.
        p. cm—(The way they play)
    Includes discographic references.
    ISBN 0-87930-761-7 (alk. paper)
    1. Guitar—Instruction and study. 2. Rock music—Instruction and study.
    3. Guitarists—Biography. I. Maloof, Rich. II. Title. III. Series.

    MT580.N47 2003
    787.87'166—dc22

                                                            2003052394

Printed in the United States of America
02 03 04 05 06   5 4 3 2 1

CONTENTS

INTRODUCTION

 Making an acoustic guitar sound good is difficult. Unadorned acoustic playing is about as naked as it gets for a guitar player, and slips, neck squeaks, missed notes, and fumbled fingerings have no place to hide.

But to make the acoustic guitar *rock* is an entirely different type of accomplishment, because it puts this box of wood and steel in a role usually occupied by an electric guitar: front and center, driving a band.

In rock music the acoustic is, to some degree, the unloved stepchild of the electric, especially when it comes to forming bands, performing on stage, or jamming with other musicians. Guitarists often think of "graduating" to the electric guitar, even though that instrument is more comfortable to handle and easier to coax cool sounds from than an acoustic. But when someone steps to centerstage with an acoustic, they're going to work.

The guitarists we've chosen for this book have all demonstrated a mastery of the acoustic guitar within the confines of rock music. They run the gamut from soft rock (James Taylor, Paul Simon) to country rock (Neil Young, the Eagles) to mainstream rock (the Rolling Stones, Dave Matthews, Tom Petty) to heavy rock (the Who) to alternative rock (R.E.M.).

We should also clarify here what this book is *not* about. It isn't about singer-song-writers, although many of our subjects have made careers as singer-songwriters. There are plenty of singer-songwriters who play guitar but haven't pushed the instrument in new directions within rock, from Bob Dylan on up to Freedy Johnston. Rest assured, if you can play the material in this book, you can tackle their guitar parts. Nor is it about rock guitarists who have shown some serious acoustic chops, such as Steve Howe and Jimmy Page, or fingerstyle virtuosos like Leo Kottke and Michael Hedges. This book is about individuals who took rock to new levels via their acoustic playing. In many cases you can even trace the acoustic lines in their electric playing as they strum and chime (almost universally) on semi-hollow Ricks and electric 12-strings.

Playing great acoustic-rock guitar is about mastering melodic and rhythmic sense, two-handed precision, and the instrument's integration with a vocal line within a band arrangement. It's about understanding the subtleties of the guitar's elements: striking some strings and not others, syncopating strokes, and even positioning your hand in front of or behind the soundhole. Without effects pedals, you have to make the guitar and your fingers provide the tone, the dynamics, and the mood of whatever you're playing.

Our intention is to offer a clear and complete picture of how these ten players do what they do best. *The Acoustic-Rock Masters* is the second book in our *The Way They Play* series, which we created so that musicians could explore the styles of these established guitarists from a variety of perspectives. We're presuming that players who read this book and learn from its examples already have a basic knowledge of the instrument. Because of that, we haven't revisited fundamental lessons or defined terms we believe you're already familiar with. Instead, we've included biographies, gear, discographies, setups, techniques, and audio samples that characterize each player's approach.

More people own acoustic guitars than any other instrument in the world. There's something to be said for that. There's also something to be said for the fact that the vast majority of those guitars are in closets getting dusty. We hope this volume encourages you to keep that guitar in the sunlight, make it sing like the masters do, and gain useful insight into the way they play.

—HP Newquist and Rich Maloof

NOTATIONAL SYMBOLS

The following symbols are used in *The Acoustic-Rock Masters* to notate fingerings, techniques, and effects commonly used in guitar music. Certain symbols are found in either the tablature or the standard notation only, not both. For clarity, consult both systems.

4● : Left-hand fingering is designated by small Arabic numerals near note heads (1=first finger, 2=middle finger, 3=third finger, 4=little finger, t=thumb).

p● : Right-hand fingering designated by letters (p=thumb, i=first finger, m=middle finger, a=third finger, c=little finger).

②● : A circled number (1–6) indicates the string on which a note is to be played.

⊓ : Pick downstroke.

Ⅴ : Pick upstroke.

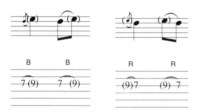

Bend: Play the first note and bend to the pitch of the equivalent fret position shown in parentheses.

Reverse Bend: Pre-bend the note to the specified pitch/fret position shown in parentheses. Play, then release to indicated pitch/fret.

Hammer-on: From lower to higher note(s). Individual notes may also be hammered.

Pull-off: From higher to lower note(s).

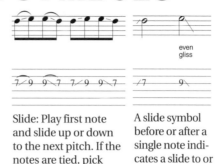

Slide: Play first note and slide up or down to the next pitch. If the notes are tied, pick only the first. If no tie is present, pick both.

A slide symbol before or after a single note indicates a slide to or from an undetermined pitch.

Finger vibrato.

Bar vibrato.

Bar dips, dives, and bends: Numerals and fractions indicate distance of bar bends in half-steps.

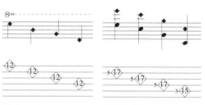

Natural harmonics.

Artificial harmonics.

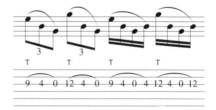

Pick-hand tapping: Notes are hammered with a pick-hand finger, usually followed by additional hammer-ons and pull-offs.

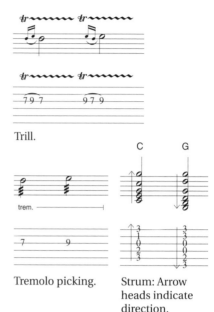

Trill.

Tremolo picking.

Strum: Arrow heads indicate direction.

HOW TABLATURE WORKS

The horizontal lines represent the guitar's strings, the top line standing for the high *E*. The numbers designate the frets to be played. For instance, a 2 positioned on the first line would mean play the 2nd fret on the first string (0 indicates an open string). Time values are indicated on the standard notation staff seen directly above the tablature. Special symbols and instructions appear between the standard and tablature staves.

CHORD DIAGRAMS

In all chord diagrams, vertical lines represent the strings, and horizontal lines represent the frets. The following symbols are used:

▬▬▬▬ Nut; indicates first position.

X   Muted string, or string not played.

○   Open string.

⌒   Barre (partial or full).

●   Placement of left-hand fingers.

ⅠⅠⅠ Roman numerals indicate the fret at which a chord is located.

Arabic numerals indicate left-hand fingering.

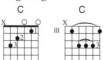

ON RECORDING ACOUSTICS

When performing live onstage, it's common for acoustic players to use onboard pickups and direct input (DI) boxes. The signal, much like an electric guitar's, is far easier to control when it's not subject to the many variables of a microphone. However, an acoustic's natural sound comes primarily off the face, or soundboard, of the guitar. This sound is very difficult to reproduce accurately with pickups. Pros have found some success with systems that blend the signals of a pickup and onboard mic. But in the controlled environment of a recording studio, they mic their instruments.

A handful of standard recording practices has emerged over the years. Of course, the only thing easier to find than an accepted convention is someone who rejects it. Methods of recording vary according to the end result sought. Before you begin, you should know what you hope to have captured when you're finished. Is it a sparkly fingerstyle sound or a warm and bassy jazz tone? Is it for solo guitar, guitar and vocals, or part of an ensemble?

To understand the variables and how you might use them to your advantage, consider the elements at work.

Guitar. High-quality guitars have good intonation, less fret noise, and a pleasing tone, and they project sound evenly across all six strings. These factors all make for better, cleaner recordings. But even the cheapest models can be put to good use. While you might not want to use a $150 guitar for a solo Celtic piece, it might be an interesting layer within an arrangement, overdriven on a rock tune, or strung up in Nashville (high-strung) tuning.

Technique. Your technique comes under the microscope on recordings. Imperfections like muted strings, string squeaks, and accidental taps on the body tend to stand out. Likewise, subtle variations—whether you play near the bridge or neck, pick with nails or flesh, or use a light or heavy pick—will be emphasized on the recording.

Mic choice. Most professionals favor small-diaphragm condenser mics for recording acoustics, and good condensers can now be had for under $400. Arguments can be made for omnidirectional versus cardioid, as well as small-diaphragm versus large-diaphragm; if you're considering a purchase, it's worth some research and testing. The use of two microphones at the same time (typically a matched pair) is common.

Mic placement. Mic techniques vary widely, though a few are especially popular. See the essay on mic placement below.

Environment. A good recording captures sound as it exists in a particular room. A heavily carpeted and draped room will result in a flat, muted sound; an all-wood room will resonate sympathetically with the guitar; a large hall or high ceiling provides natural reverberation.

Processing and mixing. There's no "fix it in the mix" solution for a poorly recorded guitar, but good processing and mixing techniques can enhance your tracks. Compressors and limiters are sometimes used to produce consistent signal levels and limit spikes in the input level; EQ can cut unwanted frequencies (typically in the mids or the "boomy" low end) or boost a desired range; delay and reverb effects can change listeners' perception of the room in which the guitar is played.

MIC PLACEMENT

Recording with two microphones allows for placement of two discrete channels of the same performance in the stereo field. Producers will sometimes create additional tracks with additional mics, by duplicating tracks, and/or by using effects returns, and then flow each signal to its own place in the stereo field.

The following techniques assume your objective is to capture the acoustic as realistically as possible. They're all subject to the idiosyncrasies of the room, the instrument, and the player. Use them as a starting point, making necessary adjustments as you see fit.

X pattern and Y pattern

For the X pattern, cross the heads of two cardioid condenser mics, one under the other, at an angle of approximately 90 degrees. One capsule should be pointed toward the bridge, the other toward the top of the guitar's neck. Set the mics 6"–10" from the guitar, between the soundhole and the neck joint.

The Y method is similar, but the mic capsules are on the same plane—angled toward one another and almost touching. The shape is more like a V than a Y.

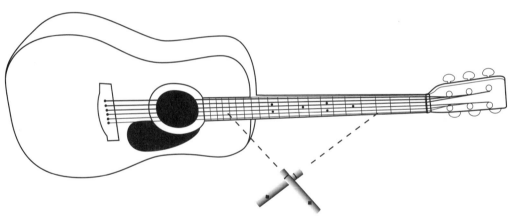

The X pattern, in which the mic tips are crossed.

The Y pattern, with the mic tips almost touching.

The objective in both these methods is to capture a sweet spot, where the low-end boom of the soundhole is offset by the brighter, thinner tones coming off the neck.

These are both reliable methods and are designed for stereo recording, so pan the mics hard left and hard right. However, since the mics are collecting sound in the same place, the stereo split is somewhat compromised.

Single mics

Place an omnidirectional mic at least 6" out from the high end of the neck, and angle it toward the soundhole. The omni, so named because it picks up sound from the entire surrounding sphere, will pick up sound from the neck, the soundhole, and some of the surrounding room.

You can use a cardioid mic to similar effect. However, a cardioid picks up sound in a heart-shaped pattern; since it rejects sound behind the tip, less tone coming off the neck—and less room—will be in the signal.

A single omni mic.

THE WAY THEY SOUND
More Recording Tips

- New strings are usually best for recording.
- The attack of a pick on the strings hits the same EQ range as a drummer's hi-hat. Utilize the percussive aspect of a strummed guitar.
- Alternate tunings change the frequencies that are projected; mic placement may need adjusting.
- A wound 3rd string projects more sound and stays in tune better than an unwound string.

- Have someone else play your guitar so you know what it sounds like. Where the performer hears the instrument—above and behind the upper bout—is an inaccurate position from which to judge a guitar's sound.
- Many players stack tracks, with additional guitars playing different chord voicings. It may be impossible to emulate the tone you hear on record with a single guitar.
- Miking too closely or directly at the soundhole will result in low-end "boom." Trying backing off or aiming the mic off axis.

"3:1" separated pairs

Use two mics, one pointed at the 12th fret and one pointed at the bridge. The 3:1 ratio determines distance: The space between the mics should be at least three times the distance between each mic and the guitar. For instance, if one mic is 6" from the bridge, the other mic should be at least 18" away (and 6" from the 12th fret).

The mics need not be on the same plane, but the 3:1 rule should still be applied. One mic can hang from above, level with the player's head and pointing back toward the guitar.

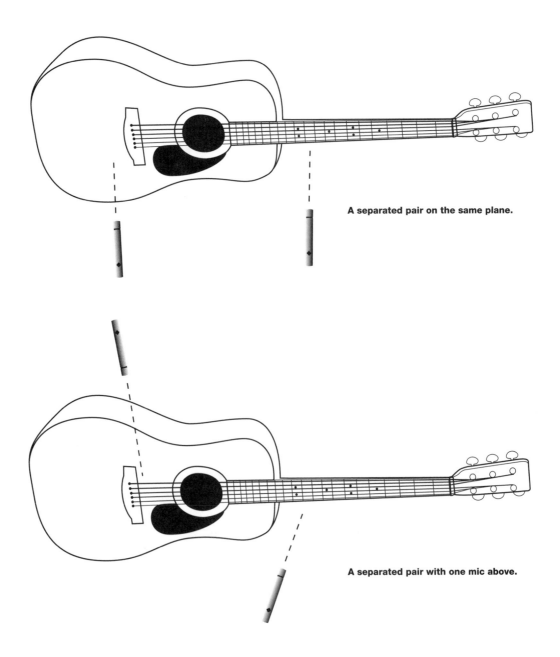

A separated pair on the same plane.

A separated pair with one mic above.

Room mic

Room mics are sometimes used in addition to, but not in place of, those mics placed close to the guitar. They provide the room's aural atmosphere, naturally delayed signals, and extra tracks to place in a mix. Also, room mics can help solve the problems of "proximity effect," in which bass response is exaggerated nearer the source. All microphones are prone to the proximity effect. Mics placed farther away will be brighter and catch frequencies the close mics cannot.

Set up two mics, one in line with the headstock and one with the tailpin, 2'–4' from the guitar.

Single mics or stereo pairs can be set up most anywhere in a room, to varying effect.

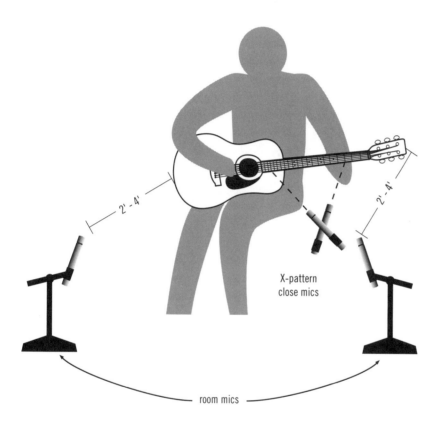

A pair of room mics added to an X-pattern setup.

CHAPTER 1 Neil Young

No guitarist has so deftly moved between the electric and acoustic worlds as Neil Young. Both a certified founder of country folk-rock and the acknowledged "Godfather of Grunge," Young changes guitar styles as frequently as most players change strings. His disregard for the conventions of guitar technique have created a sound and style that is at once ragged and pristine, and among the most accessible of any popular musician's.

BIOGRAPHY

Born on November 12, 1945, in Toronto, Canada, Neil Young lived most of his childhood in Winnipeg. The rural town's isolation had much in common with the American West, complete with its own variation of country and folk music. Young picked up the guitar in high school and immediately started writing his own songs. He put together an early rock band called the Esquires while indulging his acoustic side by playing in folk clubs. A relentlessly restless individual, Young moved to Toronto in his late teens to try his hand as a solo folksinger.

His travels brought him into contact with a diverse group of fellow musicians, including Stephen Stills, Joni Mitchell, and Rick James (later of "Super Freak" fame). Young and James formed a band with bassist Bruce Palmer called the Mynah Birds, and they signed with Motown Records. With James busted for draft evasion and their record going nowhere anyway, Young and Palmer drove to Los Angeles in Young's car, an old hearse. In L.A. they met up with Stephen Stills—legend has it Stills and guitarist/vocalist Richie Furay recognized Young's hearse at a traffic light—and formed Buffalo Springfield in 1967. Blending acoustic folk with a light electric-rock sound, the band established itself as a crucial part of the nascent California country folk-rock movement. Buffalo Springfield (named after a steamroller manufacturer) blended Young's primitive guitar approach with Stills's more polished playing, resulting in songs ranging from Stills's "For What It's Worth" to Young's innocent "I Am a Child."

The band lasted for three albums and barely two years, collapsing after friction developed between Young and Stills. Working on his own, Young turned around quickly and in 1969 released his self-titled solo debut, a commercial failure. Shifting gears, he hooked up with a band called the Rockets, and—performing as Neil Young with Crazy Horse—released *Everybody Knows This Is Nowhere*. The album became a benchmark of Young's work, matching sizzling rock songs like "Cinnamon Girl" with acoustic laments like "Down by the River." The latter song demonstrated Young's ability to take a handful of chords, lazily strummed on an acoustic, and turn them into something completely his own. Throughout his career, his best acoustic numbers would follow the same template.

Drawn again to Stephen Stills, he joined the already successful Crosby, Stills & Nash in 1970 for CSNY's *Déjà Vu*. Young's unrefined voice and elementary guitar style somehow meshed superbly with the trio's musical precision, and the album made CSNY the "supergroup" of country folk-rock. Young's standout acoustic contribution was "Helpless," which melded the lushness of the CSN core with Young's voice and plaintive guitar. Young had a rancorous falling out with the other members of CSNY, and he quit the band before the release of its live *Four Way Street* in 1971.

Young had continued to record as a solo act even during his brief CSNY tenure, releasing the most popular albums of his career, *After the Gold Rush* (1970) and *Harvest* (1972). While both records showcased Young's acoustic side, and the *Gold Rush* ballad "Only Love Can Break Your Heart" brought Young deserved fame, it was *Harvest* that cemented his reputation as the premier country folk-rocker. "Heart of Gold" and "Old Man" (featuring James Taylor on banjo) epitomized Young's playing: simple chords, simple changes, and catchy yet introspective lyrics. There was nothing flashy about his playing—if anything, it was rough around the edges—yet no one put it all together the way Young did. His almost carefree approach to guitar playing inspired countless acoustic players who found they could learn the songs on *Harvest* in a few minutes.

For the next several years Young embarked on a more eclectic electric path, spurred on by personal tragedies and his own drug use. In 1973–75 he released albums such as *Time Fades Away, Tonight's the Night,* and *Zuma,* records featuring dark songs that explored the drug overdoses and deaths of friends.

Despite his perpetually prickly relationship with Stills, the two reteamed as a duo for the country-tinged *Long May You Run* in 1976. Young left Stills in the middle of the album's tour and went solo again, crafting the rocking *American Stars 'n Bars.* That was followed by the uncharacteristically bright acoustic album *Comes A Time,* featuring the country-pop hit "Lotta Love." In 1979 Young finally found a way to bring his seemingly schizophrenic acoustic and electric sides together on the brilliant *Rust Never Sleeps.* Side One featured acoustic songs in the classic Young vein, such as "Thrasher" and "My My, Hey Hey (Into the Blue)." Side Two comprised brutal, distorted rockers, including a buzzsaw inversion of "My My, Hey Hey (Into the Blue)" called "My My, Hey Hey (Out of the Black)."

CHECKLIST ✓

Guitar . . . . Martin D-28, D-18, D-45; Taylor 12-string

Setup . . . . Low action to achieve string buzzing

Strings . . . . D'Addario light-gauge phosphor-bronze

Pickups . . . . Frap 3-axis stereo pickups

Amplification . . . Varies

Settings . . . . Varies

Effects . . . . Stereo output of top and bottom strings

Tone . . . . Straight acoustic, emphasized midrange

Picking . . . . Herco Flex 50 flat

Attack . . . . Percussive, palm-muted strum

Signature traits . . . . Simplicity, rawness

Influences . . . . . Bert Jansch, Jimi Hendrix

Overall approach . . . . . . Chameleon-like; aggressive alternating with laid-back

SELECTED DISCOGRAPHY

Everybody Knows This Is Nowhere
　　(Reprise, 1969)
After the Gold Rush (Reprise, 1970)
Harvest (Reprise, 1972)
So Far (with CSNY; Atlantic, 1974)
Zuma (Reprise, 1975)
Decade (Reprise, 1977)
Comes a Time (Reprise, 1978)
Rust Never Sleeps (Reprise, 1979)
Old Ways (Geffen, 1985)
Freedom (Reprise, 1989)
Harvest Moon (Reprise, 1992)

RECOMMENDED CUTS

"Old Man" (*Harvest; Decade*)
"Heart of Gold" (*Harvest; Decade*)
"Down by the River" (*Everybody Knows This Is Nowhere; Decade*)
"Needle and the Damage Done" (*Harvest; Decade*)
"My My, Hey Hey (Into the Blue)" (*Rust Never Sleeps*)
"Thrasher" (*Rust Never Sleeps*)
"Sugar Mountain" (*Decade*)
"I Am a Child" (*Retrospective: The Best of Buffalo Springfield*; Atco)
"Ride My Llama" (*Rust Never Sleeps*)

Apparently having resolved these conflicting sides to his satisfaction, Young spent the next decade veering all over the musical map. He recorded a country album (*Hawks & Doves*), an electronic album (*Trans*), a rockabilly album (*Everybody's Rockin'*), a new wave album (*Landing on Water*), and an R&B album (*This Note's for You*). The records alienated fans, critics, and his record company. To compound his strange musical choices, he rejoined CSNY for *American Dream* in 1989.

But that same year he released *Freedom*, featuring the anthemic "Rockin' in the Free World," a song which put him back in the pop and rock mainstream. He followed it with 1990's *Ragged Glory*—and unexpectedly found himself in the right place at the right time. Alternative and grunge rockers sang the praises of his recent records and cited the legacy of his raw, visceral early work. In an arc reminiscent of his early career, Young then forsook the electric guitar in 1992 to produce the acoustic *Harvest Moon*, an album hailed as his "*Harvest* for the '90s."

As the newly claimed mentor of the grunge set, he memorialized Kurt Cobain (*Sleeps with Angels*) and released an album with Pearl Jam (*Mirror Ball*). Even that phase didn't last long, as he worked his way back into CSNY for 1999's *Looking Forward* and its subsequent tour.

A slew of live albums and spotty studio records rounded out the 1990s. Young released *Silver and Gold* in 2000 and then *Are You Passionate?* in 2003, ensuring that his legacy, however he chooses to pursue it, continues well into this millennium.

GEAR & SETUP

Young's approach to his acoustic guitars is as idiosyncratic as his recording career has been. He's inclined to buy used guitars, believing that they've not only been seasoned and broken in, but that "they've got a song or two in them." Over the course of a single album he may use one guitar for composing and another for recording, and yet another for live performance.

Young's main acoustic guitars have always been Martins, including a D-18 from the 1930s, a D-45, and a D-28. He uses Taylor 12-strings. Young has also been known to use cheap guitars to achieve a particular tone or feel. He uses D'Angelico light-gauge strings and likes them to buzz slightly, so he sets his acoustic action lower than normal. He flatpicks using Herco Flex 50s.

Most of Young's guitars are fitted with old Frap stereo pickups. The stereo setup allows the strings to be split so that the top three strings can be panned and processed independently of the bottom three. The Fraps had three-dimensional sensing, meaning they pick up vibrations from the guitar top as well as from the bridge saddle. This provides Young with a fuller and perhaps more natural acoustic sound live. He starts with his EQ flat and adjusts it for each performance.

STYLE & TECHNIQUE

Young is one of the most accessible recording artists ever to pick up the guitar. Much of his appeal to guitarists has to be attributed to the inspiring simplicity of his playing. He relies heavily on the open-position chords that every guitarist first learns (*G, C, D, F, Am, Em*), and his strumming is consistent and rhythmic (unlike, say, that of Keith Richards). It is notable that Young can rework traditional chords and changes, along with a basic "down-down-up-up-down-up" strumming pattern, and turn them into something uniquely his own.

It is perhaps Young's disregard for the more complex and intricate possibilities of the guitar that make him so unusual. Admitting to little or no knowledge of theory, including scales or modes, he has established a narrow technique subset within which to work—and he pushes the boundaries of that format. Some argue that his lack of a polished technique is, in and of itself, a respectable technique. Decried by the speed merchants of rock for his lack of electric guitar finesse—but praised by others for infusing every note with emotional purity—Young is as influential in the realm of acoustic rock as any single artist has ever been.

The most identifiable characteristic of Young's acoustic repertoire is the way he attacks chords, which is more of a thump than a strum. Even on lead lines and double-stop figures, his parts are often driven by a percussive, rhythmic pounding of the right hand. Young brings his pick down hard on the strings while at the same time getting the meaty heel of his hand into the stroke. The result is a very strong attack that is immediately muted. He alternates these attacks, which often fall on beats *one* and *three*, with non-muted strokes on *two* and *four*. It's a unique and effective technique that builds tension, adds rhythmic punch, and brings melody notes to the foreground.

Young does much of his work tuned down a half- or a whole-step from standard. He heavily favors dropped-*D* (*DADGBE*) and double dropped-*D* (*DADGBD*), which he refers to as "*D* modal." He's also been known to lower either of these two tunings by a step.

Young is meticulous and quirky about his recording methods, frequently deciding that versions recorded during rehearsals or while practicing will be the final album cut. He maintains a studio at his Northern California ranch, which allows him to indulge in any number of variations of guitars, sounds, and recording possibilities. He claims to have a vault of nearly everything he has ever recorded—much of which has never been released commercially.

LESSON

Three characteristics immediately lend Neil Young's stamp to **Ex. 1**: the hand banging percussively on the strings and body; hammers and pulls; and a pumping, start-stop delivery. With the pick between your thumb and forefinger, relax your right hand so its heel and remaining fingers slap the guitar with every downbeat attack. The hammers are easily managed, with most executed from open strings to chord tones. Also characteristic of Young is the inclusion of a dissonant or unexpected chord into an otherwise simple progression. The tensions in the *Am*(add#5) change here make it uniquely Neil.

Ex. 1

Spending some time with Neil Young's acoustic work gives you the feeling he can play with more proficiency than he lets on. In a setting like **Ex. 2**, it's as if he deliberately avoids a clean delivery. Young's approach lends a relatively conservative part a fragile, damaged quality. Within the first two changes, a picking pattern emerges and establishes a motif. As you approach this part, note that the strings are struck on every downstroke and every upstroke. The hammer within the *Fmaj7* is a small but effective touch. Elements such as these are clearly more essential to his style than clean and precise playing.

Ex. 2

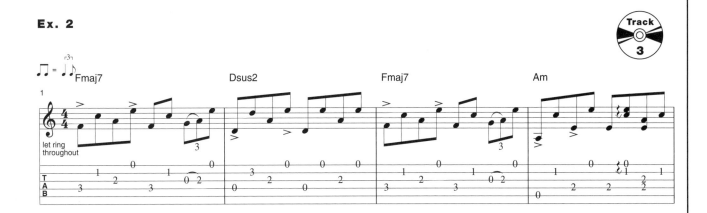

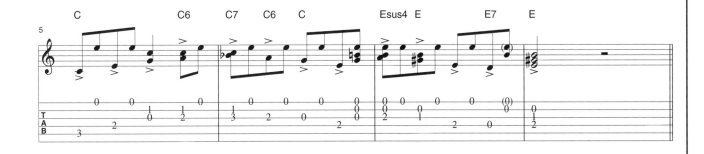

There's more than a small dose of country influence in Neil Young's acoustic work. A variation on the age-old *boom-chuck* feel is heard here, as it is throughout Young's catalog at a variety of tempos. The technique is loose, with some of the bass-note pickups ringing true and others sacrificed for feel and momentum.

Ex. 3

CHAPTER 2   George Harrison

The "quiet" Beatle was the most accomplished guitarist in a hypertalented group. While he experimented with dozens of musical forms over his 40-year career, at the heart of his playing was a strong appreciation for American country and rockabilly. He put this to superb use primarily in his solo career, where he was free to explore his acoustic voice more than he ever could in the Beatles. The result was memorable acoustic playing that represented Harrison's best work, in or out of the Beatles.

BIOGRAPHY

George Harrison was born on February 25, 1943, in Liverpool, England. He took an early interest in skiffle music, as played by Lonnie Donegan, and started playing guitar around the age of 12. While many of his peers were listening to American blues records by Robert Johnson or John Lee Hooker, Harrison was listening to country and rockabilly records by Carl Perkins, Chet Atkins, and Duane Eddy. As a result, his style of playing was more refined and less raw than that of other guitarists who would become part of the British Invasion.

Harrison was encouraged by an older classmate, Paul McCartney, to learn all he could about the guitar. At age 15 Harrison's devotion to learning his instrument paid off when he was asked to play in the Quarry Men, a band led by guitarist John Lennon and featuring McCartney. Persuaded by McCartney, Harrison passed the audition with Lennon—held late at night in the top of a double-decker bus—and the three became the core of the band. Several lineup and name changes came over the next few years before they finally gelled as the Beatles with the addition of Ringo Starr on drums in 1962. The band established itself by doing covers of rockabilly tunes by Perkins and Chuck Berry, giving their music much more of a pop feel than the gritty guitar blues favored by the Rolling Stones or the Yardbirds.

Signed to Parlophone/Capitol Records in 1962 by producer George Martin, the Beatles released their first album, *Please Please Me*, the following year. When they first came stateside and played *The Ed Sullivan Show* in 1964, the perception of the Beatles—and guitar players—was changed forever. While earlier artists like Elvis Presley had used the guitar as a prop more than anything else, the Beatles were all musicians. Their guitar-driven songs drove interest in the instrument to heights never known before.

Harrison's skill made him the de facto lead guitarist in a band where every member except Ringo was a capable guitarist. But the band was very much in the hands of Lennon and McCartney, and it was Lennon's bouncy rhythm parts and McCartney's melodic bass lines that dominated its guitar sound. Harrison's leads, and his songwriting, were relegated to the second tier of the Beatles' records. Thus, his contributions rarely stood out, with the exception of a handful of tracks like "If I Needed Someone," "Love You Too," and the edgy "Taxman."

When the band stopped touring in 1966 after nearly a decade on the road, Harrison took the opportunity to expand his horizons as both an instrumentalist and a songwriter. He developed a fluid slide technique and a light acoustic style that would define his sound going forward, taking the place of his rockabilly electric playing. He also added instruments like the sitar (inspired by Ravi Shankar, who would prove a lifelong friend) to his talents, and polished his songwriting skills.

The last few Beatles albums, notably the "White Album" (*The Beatles*) and *Abbey Road*, revealed Harrison's talents and nearly elevated him to equal status with Lennon and McCartney. Songs like "While My Guitar Gently Weeps," "Here Comes the Sun," and "Long, Long, Long" were standouts on the albums, proving that Harrison had both the songwriting and the guitar chops to be taken seriously alongside his bandmates. The last song the Beatles ever recorded was Harrison's "I Me Mine."

Harrison's newfound status as a self-sufficient performer and writer was cemented when his 1970 album, *All Things Must Pass*, became the most successful of all the Beatles' solo records. Freed of the shadow of Lennon and McCartney, Harrison put together a three-disc record that showcased all the facets of his personality, both in his life and as a guitarist. His playful, occasionally dark sense of humor emerged, his religious goals seemed to come into focus, and he exhibited an air of peace. His playing blossomed, and he displayed a compositional style that had never surfaced in the Beatles' day. The record also featured guest performances by some of the best guitarists and session players in the business. Among them was Eric Clapton, who shared a close friendship as well as a mantle of rock guitar royalty with Harrison—despite the fact that Harrison's wife left him for Clapton (a relationship that was immortalized in Clapton's "Layla"). *All Things Must Pass* contained deep, thick acoustic tracks (thanks to guest guitarists and producer Phil Spector) on tunes like "My Sweet Lord," "If Not for You," "Apple Scruffs," and "Isn't It a Pity."

The following year Harrison staged the Concert for Bangladesh, the all-star performance and three-album recording that set the stage for countless charity concerts to come. Harrison's output over the next two decades, however, was erratic. While he had a built-in fan base, his efforts seemed spectacularly unfocused. With some notable exceptions—*Living in the Material World*, *Somewhere in England*, and *Cloud Nine*—his records were neither commercially nor critically

CHECKLIST ✓

Guitar . . . . Gibson J-160E and J-200

Setup . . . . Standard

Pickups . . . . Single-coil, at tail of neck

Tone . . . . Full, covering entire range of mids

Attack . . . . Light for fingerpicking; strong for rhythm parts

Signature traits . . . . Full-arm strum; interwoven arpeggios and melodies

Influences . . . . . . Chet Atkins, Duane Eddy, Carl Perkins

Overall approach . . . . Supportive role

SELECTED DISCOGRAPHY

With the Beatles:

Rubber Soul (Capitol, 1965)

Revolver (Capitol, 1966)

Sgt. Pepper's Lonely Hearts Club Band
(Capitol, 1967)

Magical Mystery Tour (Capitol, 1967)

The Beatles (Capitol, 1968)

Abbey Road (Capitol, 1969)

Let It Be (Capitol, 1970)

Solo albums:

All Things Must Pass (Capitol, 1970)

Living in the Material World
(Capitol, 1973)

Somewhere in England
(Dark Horse, 1981)

Cloud Nine (Dark Horse, 1987)

The Traveling Wilburys, Vol. 1
(Wilbury, 1988)

RECOMMENDED CUTS

"Here Comes the Sun" (*Abbey Road*)

"Piggies" (*The Beatles*)

"While My Guitar Gently Weeps" (*The Beatles*)

"Apple Scruffs" (*All Things Must Pass*)

"My Sweet Lord" (*All Things Must Pass*)

"If Not for You" (*All Things Must Pass*)

"Handle with Care" (*The Traveling Wilburys, Vol. I*)

"Run of the Mill" (*All Things Must Pass*)

"Long, Long, Long" (*The Beatles*)

successful. He actually found more success as a film producer (especially of Monty Python movies). The most celebrated spot in his later music career was with the Traveling Wilburys, in which he teamed with Tom Petty, Bob Dylan, Roy Orbison, and Jeff Lynne as a country-rock supergroup. Primarily an acoustic outing that paid homage to their respective roots, the Wilburys' album was surprisingly successful, with Harrison contributing the folkie hit "Handle with Care." Orbison passed away within a month of the album's release, and the remaining four members released a second album two years later, to lesser acclaim.

In the late 1990s, as the surviving Beatles came to terms with their legacy and released archival material, all of the members found renewed mainstream popularity. Yet this period was marked by stunning headlines about Harrison's health and personal life. He was attacked and nearly stabbed to death by an intruder in his house in 1999. Then, after he battled throat cancer in the 1990s, news leaked to the press in 2001 that he had brain cancer. After a sustained illness, Harrison died in Los Angeles on November 29, 2001.

Producer Jeff Lynne and Harrison's son, Dhani, completed several Harrison tracks after his death to release *Brainwashed* in 2002.

GEAR & SETUP

Harrison's very first guitar was a cheap Egmond flat-top acoustic made in the Netherlands. By the time he joined the Quarry Men, he had stepped up to a Hofner President. In the Beatles he and John Lennon had matching Gibson J-160E acoustics equipped with single-coil pickups as well as tone and volume pots.

It was with a Gibson J-200 that Harrison recorded his standout tracks on the "White Album": "Piggies," "While My Guitar Gently Weeps," and "Long, Long, Long." He would rely on the instrument's big-bodied sound for the rest of his career.

While he was in the Beatles, Harrison used to remove the paint and varnish from many of his guitars. He stated that when a guitar is stripped to the bare wood, "it seems to sort of breathe." His taste for acoustic timbres presumably influenced his electric choices as well, evidenced in the semi-acoustic Gretsches and Rickenbackers with which he is closely associated.

Harrison played a Ramirez nylon-string classical, as seen in the film *A Hard Day's Night*. He and the rest of the band shared a Framus Hootenanny 12-string that can be heard on "Help!" and "You've Got to Hide Your Love Away" (in dropped-*D* tuning). He also recorded with a variety of other stringed instruments, including ukuleles and sitars.

It's well documented that George Martin's creative production and arrangements were as essential to the Beatles' sound as were the musical performances. While Harrison's acoustic was subjected to occasional studio experimentation, it benefited from Martin's discretion in recreating it as purely and unadorned as possible. Phil Spector, who produced *All Things Must Pass*, also was careful in capturing the quality of Harrison's performances. Though famous for his "wall of sound" productions, Spector used a simple and organic technique to create the immensely rich acoustic sound on tracks like "My Sweet Lord": guest guitarists were miked up and strummed along with Harrison—with the group of them sitting inside a huge plywood box.

STYLE & TECHNIQUE

Harrison was a fan of skiffle music, which, in its UK form, had elements of American folk and blues. Similar to jug-band music, it could be played with simple carry-along instruments (guitar, washboard, kazoo) and required that all the participants play as a group to put forth a song for dances or parties. Harrison was so adept at integration—bettering an arrangement with an in-between line, improving compositions with subtle melodies and passing phrases—that the influence of skiffle should not be underrated.

Yet Harrison's acoustic style owes more to American country and rockabilly than any other source, including folk or the blues. He favored the wide-open strumming of country music that supported the vocalist rather than standing on its own (which may explain his decision to record so few instrumentals). Songs like "My Sweet Lord," "I'd Have You Anytime," and "Apple Scruffs" are perfect examples of this approach, utilizing a full-arm strumming technique that is smooth and consistent, with few rhythmic changes or variations in the pattern.

What makes Harrison so distinctive is his use of the guitar as the foil for the vocal line or for other parts within an arrangement. Whether out front in "Here Comes the Sun" or supporting the drums in "Can't Buy Me Love," Harrison's acoustic takes the prize for best supporting role. The individual parts may not stand out on their own, but they enhance and support to the point of being indispensable. The mid-voice line woven into Lennon's "Dear Prudence," the four-note motif of "And I Love Her," the Nashville-tuned guitar noodling throughout "Run of the Mill" . . . these are the marks of a tasteful, world-class guitarist.

LESSON

Harrison can be heard doing a full-arm swing throughout his career. His fondness for the technique is clear in his solo work but is evident as early as "And I Love Her." Strum evenly, pivoting at the elbow rather than the wrist, and syncopate by catching both upstrokes and downstrokes. Harrison would often track as many as six acoustics playing simple parts like these. **Example 1** contains just two: a 6-string plus a 12-string set low in the mix. As is evident on the CD, stacking guitars does more than add weight: it emphasizes and spreads out the strummed attack. The hi-hat's timbre, which hits in the same frequency range as a strummed acoustic, is almost lost in the percussive strumming.

Ex. 1

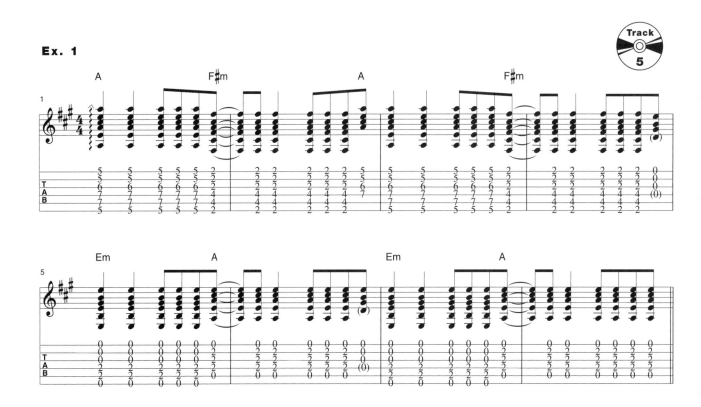

Harrison had a distinctive slide style, and though the great majority of his bottleneck is performed on electric, he occasionally utilized an acoustic. Over the same changes heard in Ex. 1, a simple slide line follows the chords in **Ex. 2**. The slide is doubled, like the strummed acoustics. Small variations where the two slides don't precisely match add to the loose, homespun feel. A little fretty slide noise doesn't hurt much, but do use proper technique and damp the strings behind the slide; for example, if you're wearing the slide on your ring finger, let your index and middle fingers ride along the strings in parallel.

Ex. 2

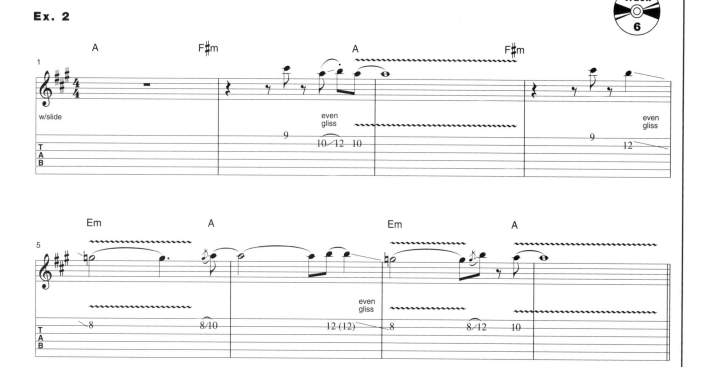

The uptempo **Ex. 3**, typical of parts Harrison played in the Wilburys and elsewhere, relies on accurate fretting and a metronomic right hand. The entrance to each chord change is anticipated every time, requiring quick fingering. The change drops faster than usual, and you have to be there to catch it.

Ex. 3

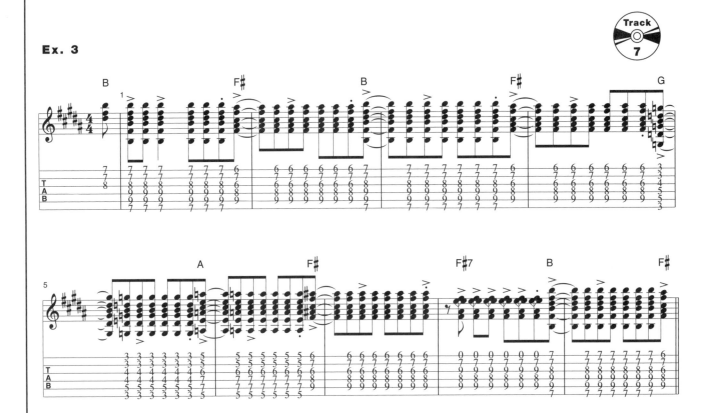

There aren't many examples of fingerpicking in George Harrison's career; in the Beatles, most fingerpicking was done by McCartney or Lennon—no doubt a songwriter's indulgence. But when he did put down the pick, Harrison had a distinct and sweet style. Much of the character in his fingerpicking work came from twisting together single- and double-note plucks, as shown in **Ex. 4**.

Track 8

Ex. 4

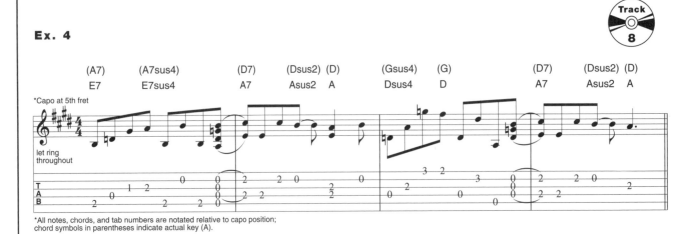

*All notes, chords, and tab numbers are notated relative to capo position;
chord symbols in parentheses indicate actual key (A).

CHAPTER 3 Paul Simon

Paul Simon is that rare acoustic player who has successfully created music in a wide range of styles and genres. Over a career spanning nearly 50 years, Simon has built on the folk roots that made him famous to become a player well versed in styles as disparate as traditional fingerpicking, reggae, and jazz, and on to African and Latin.

BIOGRAPHY

Paul Simon was born in 1941 in Queens, New York. By the time he was a teenager, Simon was writing pop songs in the vein of popular acoustic acts like the Everly Brothers. In high school he met Art Garfunkel, a singer with a high tenor voice. The two formed a group they named Tom & Jerry—after the fighting cat and mouse cartoon characters—and recorded a Simon song called "Hey Schoolgirl." To his own surprise, the song actually charted in 1957. Simon was only 16 years old.

The Tom & Jerry duo was only one of the teenaged Simon's musical pursuits. He also recorded under the pseudonym Jerry Landis and played in a band called Tico and the Triumphs. But it was his work with Garfunkel that attracted the most attention, and the two became staples of the Greenwich Village folk scene. They signed to Columbia in 1964 and, using their real names, released *Wednesday Morning, 3 AM*—which flopped so badly that the duo broke up. Simon moved to England, playing folk clubs and continuing to write songs. There he was exposed to traditional British and Celtic folk songs along with the intricate finger-picking styles of people like Davy Graham and Bert Jansch. CBS signed Simon as a solo artist, and his first album, *The Paul Simon Songbook*, was released in the UK in 1965.

A year after *Wednesday Morning* was released, producer Tom Wilson, who had been instrumental in Bob Dylan's decision to "go electric," decided to salvage one cut from Simon & Garfunkel's album. He took the acoustic tune "The Sound of Silence" and added backing tracks of electric guitar, bass, and drums—essentially adding electric rock elements. The song was released as a single and hit No. 1 on the U.S. pop charts. Its success prompted Simon to move back to America to reunite with Garfunkel.

Riding the wave of popular folk, the two became one of the most successful groups of the 1960s. Propelled by Simon's songwriting, which included legitimately poetic lyrics and deft acoustic guitar work, everything the pair released was enormously successful. Simon proved to be an adventurous songwriter, incorporating ethnic rhythms and beats in his songs, ranging from the British madrigal of "Scarborough Fair/Canticle," with its sparkling acoustic guitar line, to the South American influence of "Cecilia."

By 1970 the duo's relationship had run its course, and after more than a decade together Simon & Garfunkel acrimoniously parted ways. Simon then dove head-long into a solo career that has now lasted for more than 30 years.

While maintaining a solid pop sensibility in his songs, Simon also indulged his interest in other musical forms and styles. His first solo hit, from 1972's *Paul Simon*, was "Mother and Child Reunion," which had a bouncing reggae beat. He continued pushing his pop boundaries with the Latin-flavored "Me and Julio Down by the Schoolyard," which became an AM radio staple. Additional '70s releases like *There Goes Rhymin' Simon* and *Still Crazy After All These Years* found him quenching his broad stylistic thirst with studied explorations of more styles and forms, including gospel, Dixieland, and R&B.

Subsequent releases in the 1970s and 1980s further cemented his success as a solo artist; rarely did a two-year period pass without a Simon song on the charts. While it was clear that he had no intention of looking backward, Simon did reteam with Garfunkel and fellow singer-songwriter James Taylor in 1978 to remake the song "What A Wonderful World."

His career high point came with the release of *Graceland* in 1986. Reflecting his immersion in South African music, the album also showed Simon's continued maturation as a guitarist. Whereas his guitar had been the singular instrumental focus in the early years, Simon nimbly picked and strummed within South African ensembles, and managed to turn complex African rhythms into engaging and critically lauded pop songs. His interest turned to Brazilian music with the release *The Rhythm of the Saints* in 1990. In the mid 1990s he worked on *The Capeman*, a musical based on the murder of a Hispanic youth in New York. After it flopped on Broadway, Simon quickly followed up with the Grammy-nominated recording *You're the One* in 2000.

Simon's later work has helped establish ethnic music as a pop force in America. More than any other artist—with the exception of Peter Gabriel—Simon's album releases validated the concept of "world music" and exposed millions to previously unheard musical forms and rhythms.

Today, Simon continues to tour, hooking up with Garfunkel for the occasional celebrity concert or award ceremony. His legacy has many chapters, but all of his music has been built on an intuitive understanding of the possibilities inherent in the acoustic guitar.

CHECKLIST ✓

Guitar . . . . Martin OM-42PS, Gurian 3, Yamaha LS400

Setup . . . . standard

Strings . . . . D'Addario light-gauge phosphor-bronze

Pickups . . . . Fishman Thinline Gold Plus

Amplification . . . Pendulum preamp

Settings . . . . Filtered to amplify highs, cut midrange, and add bass

Effects . . . . Unadulterated

Tone . . . . Shimmering

Picking . . . . Fingerstyle picking (Travis and Celtic styles) and strumming, usually with nails

Attack . . . . Light

Signature traits . . . . Light touch; Travis picking; in-the-pocket rhythm parts

Influences . . . . . . Davy Graham, Bert Jansch

Overall approach . . . . Studied and precise

SELECTED DISCOGRAPHY

With Simon & Garfunkel

Wednesday Morning, 3 AM
    (Columbia, 1964)
Sounds of Silence (Columbia, 1966)
Parsley, Sage, Rosemary & Thyme
    (Columbia, 1966)
Bookends (Columbia, 1968)
Bridge over Troubled Water
    (Columbia, 1970)

Solo albums:

Paul Simon (Warner Bros., 1972)
There Goes Rhymin' Simon
    (Warner Bros., 1973)
Still Crazy After All These Years
    (Warner Bros., 1975)
Graceland (Warner Bros., 1986)
The Rhythm of the Saints
    (Warner Bros., 1990)

RECOMMENDED CUTS

(Most available on Simon & Garfunkel and Paul Simon collections)

"Anji" (*Sounds of Silence*)
"Scarborough Fair/Canticle"
    (*Parsley, Sage, Rosemary & Thyme*)
"The Sound of Silence" (*Wednesday
    Morning, 3 AM*)
"Mrs. Robinson" (*Bookends*)
"America" (*Bookends*)
"I Am a Rock" (*Sounds of Silence*)
"El Condor Pasa (If I Could)"
    (*Bridge over Troubled Water*)
"Kathy's Song" (*Sounds of Silence*)
"Something So Right" (*There Goes
    Rhymin' Simon*)
"Kodachrome" (*There Goes Rhymin'
    Simon*)

GEAR & SETUP

During the 1960s Simon used Guilds and a Martin D-18 and D-35. For the next two decades his acoustic guitars were small-bodied custom-made Yamaha LS400s (Yamaha's FJ681 was a Paul Simon signature guitar). These were built with a True Tone pickup system installed, but Simon modified them for stage use by adding internal mics.

Since the mid 1990s Simon has been touring with a Martin OM-42, custom made for him by the manufacturer. The company also produced a limited-edition Paul Simon Signature model in 1997—the OM42-PS. The small body and long scale length serve Simon's tastes as a fingerstylist. In 2002 Martin introduced a scaled-down signature model, the PS2.

Simon's other guitars, including his Ovation, are outfitted with Fishman Thinline Gold Plus pickups and D'Addario light-gauge phosphor-bronze strings. He has also used a Parker Fly, a solidbody electric that provides acoustic tones with the help of an onboard piezo pickup.

Simon does most of his recording with a Size 3 Gurian guitar, which he claims he will never modify as the sound and feel are perfect for his studio needs. He also sets up Martin acoustics for Nashville-tuned studio overdubs, to create a delicate counterbalance to the Gurian. He prefers this approach to using a 12-string. (In Nashville tuning, also known as high-stringing, the first two strings remain at standard pitch, while strings 4–6 are an octave higher. To achieve the tuning, take the higher-octave strings from a 12-string set and use them to string a 6-string instrument.) He uses nylon-string Velasquez classical guitars. Having admitted to hand strain when shifting from the wide neck of classical guitars back to the thinner necks of steel-strings, he naturally favors the latter.

Simon used a capo for much of his Simon & Garfunkel work. It was a concession to Garfunkel's high tenor, but he claims that he'd rather not use them as he prefers to play below the 5th fret.

Because he alternates between strumming and picking while playing, Simon rarely uses a pick, relying instead on strong fingernails. He treats them regularly with acrylic polish to keep them in shape.

STYLE & TECHNIQUE

Paul Simon's guitar playing is informed by a broad, multi-instrumentalist understanding of harmony and technique. His extensive musical vocabulary grows as he explores new styles, and he respectfully recreates the styles of each genre with genuine comprehension. While he'll farm out electric-guitar duties to first-call session players, Simon has always reserved the acoustic playing for himself.

He is a formidable fingerstylist, as evidenced early on with his rendition of "Anji," the acoustic solo made famous by noted British guitarist Davy Graham. Simon's acumen with Travis picking, in particular, has provided the backbone for some of his finest tunes and is in best evidence on "The Boxer." The majority of Simon & Garfunkel's hits—"Homeward Bound," "The Sound of Silence," "Scarborough Fair"—feature his steady, even fingerpicking and little else. While these selections are played predominantly with moving open-position forms against moving bass lines, Simon utilizes the length of the guitar's neck. Occasionally, as in the gorgeous "American Tune," Simon employs fingerstyle, strums, and chord melody within a single song.

Simon has a nimble right hand, and his wrist swings as if on ball bearings when he uses a pick. Classics like "Me and Julio" and "Kodachrome" feature his syncopated strumming, with a light pick emphasizing the percussive scratch across the strings. His sense of syncopation was put to the test when he played acoustic among the intricate beats and oddball time signatures of South African music on *Graceland*.

Simon has studied guitar for years with jazz guitarist Howard Morgen, and the relationship has presumably fed Simon's capabilities not only on the guitar but in composition and arranging. Well-mapped voice leadings and jazz-based harmonies infuse much of his writing, and sophisticated progressions often support even his straightforward pop outings.

LESSON

Like all the best songwriters, Simon is adept at establishing a hook within very few beats. In **Ex. 1** the guitar part introduces an instrumental hook before any other part—including vocals or melody—is even presented. A part like this could be used on most any three-chord figure. This motif is characteristic of Simon's mid-'70s career, but it presages rhythms and guitar parts heard on his South African– and Brazilian-inspired albums.

Ex. 1

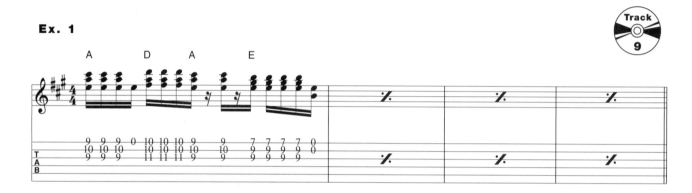

Paul Simon can Travis-pick with the best of them, and he uses the technique in both backing and solo parts. His form is orthodox: The first three fingers on your right hand should never leave respective positions on the top three strings: ring finger on the *E* string, middle on *B*, index on *G*. The thumb covers the lower three strings, hammering out an alternating bass line in eighth-notes. In **Ex. 2**, on the *Dm* chord the line does not alternate, though the steady eighth-note rhythm is maintained. The spacey *Dadd4/A* chord hangs the progression in mid-air for a bar before returning to *C*, the example's home base.

Ex. 2

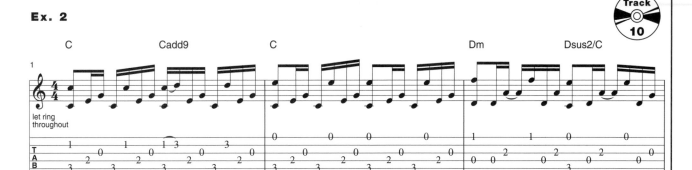

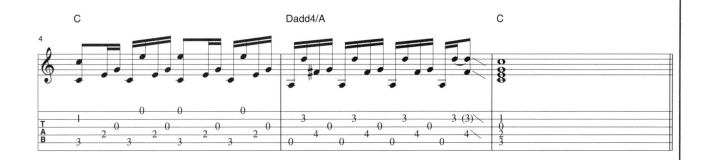

Just as Simon can make the most of a three-chord wonder, he is capable of complex composition and arranging. The few bars in **Ex. 3** rely on sophisticated chording, voice leading, and tension to make an otherwise simple transition from key to key. When all is said and done, we've simply moved from *A* to *E*—but Simon takes the long way around. The example opens with a bluesy lick, and then uses common tones to sink into warm jazz changes. (Note that the click track cuts off in the last bar to allow for the ritard.)

Ex. 3

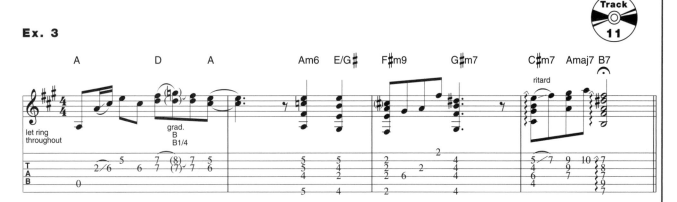

CHAPTER 4 Keith Richards

One of the stalwarts of the British rock invasion of the mid-1960s, Keith Richards has long been associated with the nasty snarl of his Fender Telecaster. But Richards brought an acoustic sensibility to rock 'n' roll that few of his contemporaries could match. He often composed on the acoustic and used its ringing tones as the basis for some of the Rolling Stones' best songs—be they ballads or blistering rockers. Even today, Richards spends most of his time recording and practicing with an acoustic guitar.

BIOGRAPHY

Keith Richards was born on December 18, 1943, in Dartford, Kent, England. His early interest in music was fueled first by a love of cowboy singer Roy Rogers, and then his grandfather prompted him to take up the guitar. Like many of his British art school peers, Richards became enamored of American blues, learning songs by Lead Belly and Robert Johnson from vinyl imports. He learned these songs on an acoustic, since that is how they were originally recorded.

In 1960 Richards joined former schoolmate Mick Jagger's band in what would soon become the Rolling Stones. With fellow guitarist Brian Jones, bassist Bill Wyman, and drummer Charlie Watts, the band gained notoriety after it landed the coveted house band gig at London's Crawdaddy Club. The Stones' popularity was due in equal parts to their electric covers of gutbucket blues and their bad-boy posturing—both of which positioned them as the urban counterpart to the clean-scrubbed and pop-oriented Beatles.

While the Stones' stage show required the unbridled energy of amplified and distorted electric guitars, Richards chose to use an acoustic for the band's early song-writing and studio sessions. Songs like "Play with Fire," "Mother's Little Helper," and "As Tears Goes By" featured his unadorned acoustic guitar in a rock band context. More interestingly, harder-edged numbers like "Street Fighting Man" and "Jumpin' Jack Flash" were also acoustic-based, their overdriven sound created by a Gibson Hummingbird with a small microphone shoved into its soundhole. Layers of electrics were later added by Richards and Brian Jones, but the core of the songs was built on the jangly resonance of Richards's acoustic.

Richards discovered alternate tunings in 1968, inspired by Don Everly's playing in the Everly Brothers. Enthusiastic about pushing outside the boundaries of concert tuning, he got tuning tips from Ry Cooder, Taj Mahal, and Gram Parsons. Open E, open D, open G, and Nashville tuning all became standards in his repertoire (see Style & Technique). To elicit sound from just those strings he wanted to hear, Richards took to removing the 6th string (low E) from his guitars.

CHECKLIST ✓

Guitar . . . . Gibson Hummingbird, Gibson L1, Martins

Setup . . . . Five strings; medium to high action

Tone . . . . Midrange, often possessing electric characteristics

Picking . . . . Usually flatpicked, occasional fingerpicking

Attack . . . . Aggressive

Signature traits . . . . Open tunings, 5-string setup

Influences . . . . . Jimmy Reed, Hank Williams, Don Everly, Chuck Berry, Muddy Waters, John Lee Hooker, Howlin' Wolf, Gram Parsons

Overall approach . . . . Reverent and raw

The original Stones' lineup changed when Brian Jones was replaced by Mick Taylor in 1969 (Jones drowned shortly thereafter). Taylor had established himself as a lead guitarist with blues bands in London, and his playing style edged Richards into a more rhythmic role. It also allowed Richards's interest in other styles of acoustic music to come to the fore. Taylor's first album with the band, *Let It Bleed*, featured acoustic numbers such as "Country Honk," "Love in Vain," and "You Can't Always Get What You Want."

By this time, however, Richards was on a personal roller coaster. Drug busts and addiction were an increasingly high-profile part of his life, as was the decision to drop the "s" from his last name (because he thought it sounded cooler). Jagger, for his part, started spending more time away from the Stones, making his first forays into acting. As such, the next album, 1971's *Sticky Fingers*, featured Richards in the band's driver's seat, and he indulged his acoustic playing to its full extent. From the acoustic strumming of "Wild Horses" (actually played by Taylor) and "Sister Morphine" to the muted picking of "Moonlight Mile" on to the acoustic slide playing on Mississippi Fred McDowell's "You Gotta Move," Richards used the acoustic as much as the electric. Never before had the band so perfectly integrated all the facets of the guitar.

The 1972 follow-up, *Exile on Main St.*, was to be one of the last multi-layered albums of the Stones' career, with acoustic numbers like "Sweet Black Angel" and "Sweet Virginia" sitting alongside rockers like "Happy" and "Tumbling Dice." Taylor left after 1974's *It's Only Rock and Roll*, replaced a year later by Richards's longtime friend, Faces guitarist Ron Wood. But as the '70s devolved into the '80s, Richards's drug problems were no match for Jagger's decision to go disco, and the band's albums only occasionally matched the stellar work of the previous two decades.

In the mid '80s the members of the Stones took time out for various solo projects, providing an occasion for Jagger and Richards to snipe at each other in the press. The solo albums were generally subpar, although Richards's *Talk Is Cheap*, released in 1988, was arguably the best of the lot. He indulged his passion for honky-tonk and swaggering blues, then toured with his band, the X-pensive Winos.

The Stones spent most of the 1990s coasting through recording sessions while mounting huge stadium tours. Rifts within the band—including Bill Wyman's departure—manifested themselves on record, and no single album stood out as a great representation of Richards's innate guitar sensibility. There were, fortunately, a couple of bright spots. *Dirty Work* featured "One Hit (to the Body)," in which Keith managed to fuse electric and acoustic seamlessly in a single gritty rocker. Then there was "Thru and Thru," from 1994's *Voodoo Lounge*, which despite its relative obscurity may be the quintessential Keith Richards tune. With its languorous acoustic and electrics meshing with heavy drums (and Keith's solo vocals), it's a perfect example of the varied elements Richards was capable of putting into a song.

The Stones still release records, which seem to serve primarily as reasons to stage another enormodrome tour. The fact that the band and its members have survived for 40 years—literally, in Richards's case—is a testament to their songwriting and performing skill. The Stones' catalog is so vast—they've produced the equivalent of two albums a year for 20 years—that most people only know their rock 'n' roll radio hits, leaving much of Richards's great acoustic work hidden. Granted, there was a lot of throwaway material buried deep on many of those albums. But any close examination of the Stones' catalog reveals that a huge chunk of it is based on Richards's love of the acoustic guitar.

GEAR & SETUP

Richards's use of equipment is perhaps the biggest mixed bag in the history of modern music. While favoring old Gibson and Martin acoustics, he has been known to pick up whatever happens to be lying around the studio if it gives him the sound he's looking for. Over the years he's had a large number of his guitars get stolen or lost, or just fall apart. He and Jagger regularly swap guitars out of their respective collections. The only constant appears to be Richards's interest in older Gibson Hummingbirds, which he used for much of the Stones' early records.

Because he's particular about sound, Richards's miking and amp setups change from album to album and even from song to song. He has admitted to having to start from scratch each time he records because he can't remember the setups he used previously. He has been known to walk into an empty studio or empty auditorium and snap his fingers to determine mic and amp placement based on the room's natural reverb. His recording techniques include toying with mic positioning, placing amps in a room, using multiple mics, cramming microphones into soundholes, using direct input, and most any other technique he feels will help the sound.

STYLE & TECHNIQUE

Richards removes the 6th string on some of his guitars because he feels it's better to dispense with the rumbling low string than to try to make it work when it's not needed, which he often finds to be the case with open tunings. His favorite tunings are (low to high) open *G* (*DGDGBD*), open *E* (*EBEG♯BE*), open *D* (*DADF♯AD*), and Nashville tuning (replacing the bottom four strings with their higher-octave counterparts).

He also uses a capo so he can shift keys in open tuning. Capoing an open *G* on the 5th fret, for instance, produces an open *C*. When playing in an open tuning, he occasionally muffles unused strings with his fretting-hand fingers.

Much of the signature Richards sound comes from the sometimes off-kilter rhythms he employs—it's been said that drummer Charlie Watts follows Keith, not the other way around—which seem perfectly in step with his own careening swagger. He will employ repeated upstrokes to emphasize the higher notes rather than slash down on the lower strings. In a move many would find counterintuitive, he tends to interrupt the up/down motion of his right arm in midstroke, reversing direction or simply stopping to let the partial stroke ring out. With this rhythmic technique, Richards gets great mileage out of simple I–IV chord changes.

As one might guess, there are only two rules in Richards's book: "Be natural" and "Ignore the rules." Still, Richards has profound respect for blues tradition; rather than reinvent the blues on his acoustic, he is always mindful of paying tribute by emulation. The open tunings he favors allow him to employ age-old fingerstyle blues techniques in a rock 'n' roll setting. As an admirer of country and rockabilly players, his strumming on the Stones' country tunes falls squarely within traditional technique, with plucked bass notes alternating with full-stroke strums. He is a refreshingly uninhibited player, so if there's a third rule in there, it's "Make loud mistakes."

Keith would just as soon pick up an acoustic as an electric for a hard-rock number, and the presence of a steady rhythm section allows him great leeway for inserting his rhythmic jabs and curt leads.

OPEN TUNINGS: SELECTED CUTS

Open *G*
"Brown Sugar" (*Sticky Fingers*)
"Can't You Hear Me Knocking" (*Sticky Fingers*)
"Honky Tonk Women" (*Through the Past, Darkly [Big Hits, Vol. 2]; ABKCO, 1969*)
"I Just Want to See His Face" (*Exile on Main St.*)
"Shake Your Hips" (*Exile on Main St.*)
"Soul Survivor" (*Exile on Main St.*)
"Start Me Up" (*Tattoo You; Virgin, 1981*)
"Tumbling Dice"; capo 4th fret (*Exile on Main St.*)
"Ventilator Blues" (*Exile on Main St.*)

"Moonlight Mile" (*Sticky Fingers*)
"Wild Horses" (*Sticky Fingers*)

Open *E*
"You Can't Always Get What You Want" (*Let It Bleed*)
"Jumpin' Jack Flash"; capo 2nd fret (*Through the Past, Darkly [Big Hits, Vol. 2]; ABKCO, 1969*)

Open *D*
"Child of the Moon" (*More Hot Rocks [Big Hits and Fazed Cookies]; ABKCO, 1971*)
"Street Fighting Man" (*Beggars Banquet*)

LESSON

Among Richards's favorite alternate tunings are open *D* (*DADF#AD*) and open *E* (*EBEG#BE*, or open *D* one whole-step up). Both facilitate easy barring and put otherwise unreachable harmonies within fingering range. **Example 1** is a characteristically aggressive rock strum between the I chord and the IVadd9. Notice that Richards establishes a feel, though not a pattern—the rhythms are different in every measure. Accents mark the upbeats that give the part its momentum and Stonesy swagger. Remember that Richards most often plays with the lowest string removed; be sure to keep your 6th string muted if you're leaving it on.

Ex. 1

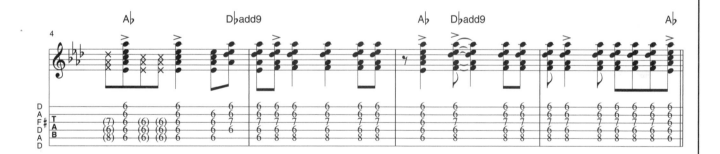

The same two changes approached from a new perspective yield completely new possibilities. Rather than barring straight across the open-tuned strings to form the I chord, **Ex. 2** uses the capo. For this ballad setting we'll start higher on the neck to get the benefit of high ringing strings, much as Nashville tuning does.

Again, use the open *D* tuning, and capo at the 9th fret. The open strings now form the I chord, *B*. The IVadd9 chord, *Eadd9*, is in the simple shape of an open-position *E7*. This example starts on the IVadd9 after a nice little pull-off move (start on an upstroke to get the most of the pull-off). Hammers and pulls continue to tie the changes together.

Ex. 2

Open D tuning
*Capo at 9th fret

*All notes, chords, and tab numbers are notated relative to capo position;
chord symbols in parentheses indicate actual key (B).

A long-avowed lover of the blues, Richards brings legitimate blues techniques and songsmithing to several acoustic numbers in the Stones' catalog. In the style of his Southern-blues predecessors, tune to open G (*DGDGBD*) for **Ex. 3**. Again, take care to remove or mute the lowest string, as it won't be used here.

The opening measure relies on the 5th and 4th strings, with the open 5th establishing a drone and a patient, melancholy figure riding along the 4th string. In the brief jump to the 4th and 3rd strings (bar 2), the drone effect continues with the open 4th string, *D*. Open *G* allows the two-bar melody to then repeat with open strings ringing. The figure plays out with a somewhat plodding strum on straight barres before a brief riff leads to the resolution.

Ex. 3

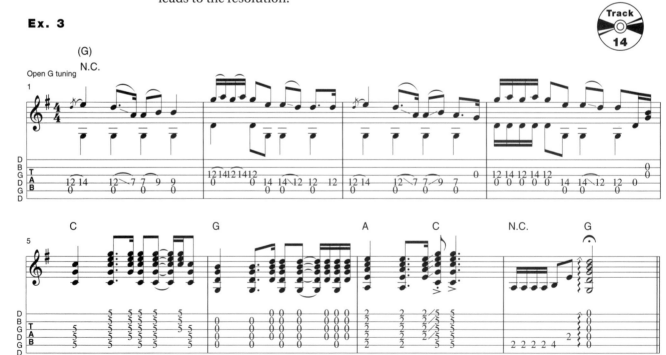

CHAPTER 5 James Taylor

James Taylor's musical success is rooted in a stellar combination of singing, songwriting, and acoustic guitar playing. His songs often tell tales of personal trials and loneliness—songs befitting a minor key—yet he offsets his lyrics with bright major chords and sparkling fingerpicking. The result is a melancholy optimism that is Taylor's stock in trade, and one that is uniquely his. As one of the elder statesman of soft rock, Taylor has a deft acoustic guitar touch that is as recognizable today as it was when he dominated radio playlists 30 years ago.

BIOGRAPHY

James Taylor was born on March 12, 1948, in Boston but was raised in Chapel Hill, North Carolina. The music in his house was steeped in Americana, from Stephen Foster to Aaron Copland to the country players of the Appalachians—music that would profoundly influence his songwriting and playing in the years to come. Taylor's early fondness for folk (Tom Rush, Elizabeth Cotton, Richard and Mimi Fariña) has informed his playing through his career.

The first instrument Taylor played was the cello, but when he was 12 his parents bought him an acoustic guitar (which his brother spray-painted blue). He spent the next four years immersed in the instrument, teaching himself to play and making up his own chord fingerings to mimic the songs he heard. To this day, he still plays some basic chords with unusual fingerings.

Taylor spent his summers in Martha's Vineyard, where he struck up a friendship with Danny Kortchmar, who would later find fame as one of L.A.'s most in-demand session guitarists, ultimately backing many of the singers and bands influenced by Taylor. Kortchmar was a blues aficionado who introduced Taylor to the music of bluesmen like Muddy Waters, Lightnin' Hopkins, Howlin' Wolf, and John Lee Hooker. Taylor and Kortchmar formed a duo called James & Kootch that performed blues and folk songs in and around Boston.

An admittedly troubled and lonely teenager, Taylor started using his guitar as an outlet for his emotions. During high school he was sent to a Massachusetts boarding school where he had to attend chapel several times a week. One benefit was that he was exposed to church hymns and found them easy to play on the guitar. He learned how to add a thumbpicked bass line—his own form of Travis picking—to fill out the majestic sound of these traditional songs.

But school bored Taylor, and he dropped out at 17 to move to New York City. That same year he was diagnosed as suicidal and sent to McLean Psychiatric Hospital in Massachusetts. After a ten-month stay he returned to Greenwich Village, the epicenter of the folk and activist movement in the mid '60s. Unfortunately, he was in the right place at the wrong time. He put together a rock band called the Flying Machine with his old friend Kortchmar. The band made a series of demos, released a single, and broke up within a year. Shortly afterward, Taylor fell into a heroin addiction that lasted until 1983.

After his failed attempt to become part of the Village scene, Taylor moved to England, where he hoped his brand of guitar playing and storytelling might be better received. After a chance meeting with Paul McCartney, Taylor became the first artist signed to the Beatles' Apple Records, which proved to be a mixed blessing. The Beatles were imploding, as was the Apple organization, and Taylor's record—despite an early version of "Carolina in My Mind"—came and went with barely a whimper. He moved back to the U.S. in 1969, and, after another stay in a mental hospital, broke both of his hands in a motorcycle accident. Things were not looking good.

Yet his one record for Apple led to interest from Warner Bros. The label signed him to a U.S. deal at the end of 1969, and the following year he released *Sweet Baby James*. The album's earthy acoustic songs—including "Fire and Rain," "Country Road," and the title track—became radio staples during 1970, heralding Taylor as the archetypal soft-rocker for a generation that embraced the style.

His cover of Carole King's "You've Got a Friend" on 1971's *Mud Slide Slim and the Blue Horizon* was a model of his musical approach. Taking another writer's song—a tune not written on a guitar—Taylor was able to create a guitar part that mimicked the ten-fingered complexity of a piano with smooth and crystalline clarity. This set Taylor apart from his peers; his ability to both interpret other artists' songs and create distinctive guitar parts would bring him success over and over again.

From 1971 onward, Taylor's career, and his style of music, remained as stable as any artist's of his generation. By the time Warner Bros. released *Greatest Hits* in the fall of 1976, Taylor had racked up eight Top 40 hits. The collection has since sold in excess of 11 million copies. His albums throughout the rest of the 1970s and '80s mined the same vein of love and loss, coupled with shimmering guitar—"blues songs without a blues structure," as he called it. Any changes to the music were by way of experiments in production or orchestration, but

CHECKLIST ✓

Guitar . . . . Olson SJs, cedar top and rosewood back and sides

Setup . . . . Standard

Strings . . . . Kaman Adamas light phosphor-bronze

Pickups . . . . L.R. Baggs LB6 bridge pickup

Amplification . . . Pendulum preamp

Settings . . . . Filtered to amplify highs, cut midrange, and add bass

Effects . . . . Chorus, light echo

Tone . . . . Shimmering highs, minimal midrange

Picking . . . . Travis-style thumb- and fingerpicking, with nails

Attack . . . . Light

Signature traits . . . . Hammer-ons, pull-offs, contrapuntal bass lines, suspended-tone embellishments

Influences . . . . . . Merle Travis, Elizabeth Cotton, the Beatles, Lightnin' Hopkins, John Lee Hooker, Joseph Spence, Aaron Copland

Overall approach . . . . Rolling and clear

SELECTED DISCOGRAPHY

James Taylor (Capitol, 1968)
Sweet Baby James (Warner Bros., 1970)
Mud Slide Slim and the Blue Horizon
    (Warner Bros., 1971)
Walking Man (Warner Bros., 1974)
Gorilla (Warner Bros., 1975)
Greatest Hits (Warner Bros., 1976)
JT (Columbia, 1977)
Never Die Young (Columbia, 1988)
New Moon Shine (Columbia, 1991)
October Road (Columbia, 2002)
The Best of James Taylor
    (Warner Bros., 2003)

RECOMMENDED CUTS
(All available on *Greatest Hits*, *Greatest Hits Vol. II*, and/or *The Best of James Taylor*)
"Carolina in My Mind" (*James Taylor*)
"Sweet Baby James" (*Sweet Baby James*)
"Fire and Rain" (*Sweet Baby James*)
"Country Road" (*Sweet Baby James*)
"Mexico" (*Gorilla*)
"Shower the People" (*In the Pocket*)
"Your Smiling Face" (*JT*)
"Don't Let Me Be Lonely Tonight"
    (*One Man Dog;* Warner Bros., 1972)
"You Can Close Your Eyes" (*Mud Slide Slim and the Blue Horizon*)
"Walking Man" (*Walking Man*)
"Never Die Young" (*Never Die Young*)
"Shed a Little Light" (*New Moon Shine*)

his guitar always remained front and center. Unlike Paul Simon, who ventured outside pop, folk, and rock for inspiration later in his career, Taylor was most comfortable doing the thing he had become popular for: creating catchy, emotional, acoustic guitar–driven songs. The occasional rocker or gutsy blues was merely an indulgence.

Never a prolific artist, Taylor released only two studio albums in the 1990s, choosing live performance over the confines of the recording studio. Nonetheless, his 1997 release, *Hourglass*, won a Grammy as Best Pop Album. He returned to the studio for 2002's *October Rain* and garnered renewed interest via the release of a new greatest-hits package in 2003.

There have been personal ebbs and sales slowdowns in his 30-year career, but Taylor remains a popular artist and strong concert draw. His enduring appeal led to inductions into the Rock and Roll Hall of Fame and the Songwriters Hall of Fame in 2000. In an appearance at the Grammy Awards in February 2003, he was featured as the inspiration for a new generation of singer-songwriters.

GEAR & SETUP

Taylor was attracted to the acoustic guitar in part because it was the one instrument he could pack up and take with him anywhere he wanted to go. That stripped-down approach to gear has stayed with him his entire career.

Over the years Taylor has played a variety of acoustics by a variety of manufacturers, notably Gibson, Martin, and Yamaha. Once he could afford them, though, he opted for handmade guitars, feeling that integration of all the elements—from choice of wood to style of bracing—better suited him as a guitarist. To that end, during the 1980s he used custom guitars created by Mark Whitebook. However, Whitebook stopped making the guitars due to failing health, and Taylor went looking for a new source.

He found it in James A. Olson. Olson's guitars, made at his shop in Circle Pines, Minnesota, have been Taylor's mainstays since the early 1990s. Taylor uses Olson small jumbos (SJs), also known as parlor guitars. While originally a fan of the heavy tones of a dreadnought, Taylor now prefers his guitars to be smaller and constructed of thin wood to give them a sharper, brighter tone—without having to actually tune to a higher pitch. He occasionally uses an Olson cutaway, not for access to the upper frets—which he never uses—but because he likes the sound. He uses Kaman Adamas light phosphor-bronze strings (although he has expressed an admiration for the strings of New Jersey luthier Phillip J. Petillo).

Each of his Olsons are fitted with L.R. Baggs pickups, as Taylor does not like to mic his guitar onstage. He runs a direct line from the guitars to a Pendulum preamp with a built-in equalizer. His equalizer setting emphasizes bright treble and a small amount of bass, taking out most of the midrange. This is part of his signature sound—losing the bland midrange tones.

In the studio Taylor faces an interesting miking issue: he often sings and plays at the same time while recording, instead of tracking his vocal separately. To limit vocal bleed while still getting the most from the guitar, he records from three sources. One is the guitar's pickup, which also serves as a signal that will receive effects or enhancement once on tape. (This includes some compression as well as doubling or echo to achieve a chorus effect.) The other two sources are a pair of directional mics pointed at the guitar in an inverted V shape (heads together and barrels pointing away from each other). This miking method captures tone coming off the guitar's neck and body, usually producing a bright, live sound while minimizing vocal leak.

STYLE & TECHNIQUE

Taylor keeps it simple with standard three- and four-finger chords, typically rooted in open position. He often separates bass and treble into distinctive, interwoven lines. This approach began as improvised Travis-style picking, using his thumb and two fingers to create both a melody and a harmony. His fingers and hand are held in a classical position, floating above the strings, with his palm parallel to the guitar neck. He doesn't anchor his hand against the guitar top with his little finger as many players do.

A signature of Taylor's style is to add ornaments to fingerpicked chords with hammers and pull-offs, usually between open and fretted strings. These gentle embellishments typically incorporate a chord's suspended 2nd (sus9) and suspended 4th, and can provide tasteful leading tones and chord transitions.

The subtle bass lines Taylor incorporates also contribute greatly to his acoustic character. He will often "walk" a bass part and/or develop a low line in counterpoint to the chord changes and melody. He also likes to plant a chord's 4th or 5th degree in the root position, a major factor in the floating, nonspecific harmonic feel that characterizes so many of his songs.

To keep his nails strong he dips the tips in Superglue and then dusts them with acrylic nail powder.

He will occasionally use dropped-*D* tuning (for which he prefers a dreadnought) but stays primarily with standard tuning. He relies on a capo to accommodate comfortable singing keys, benefiting further from the delicate tones of the higher pitches.

LESSON

As far as Taylor's acoustic playing goes, **Ex. 1** is *the move*. Similar examples can be heard on dozens of his songs, and each of them immediately identifies his style. Don't throw away a single note or ornament here—the part is all about nuance and inflection. Most of the action is in the upper strings, where chord tones and suspensions are plucked crisply and matched with strong hammerons. A tiny melody emerges from the part as double-stops give way to individually picked notes.

Ex. 1

Track 15

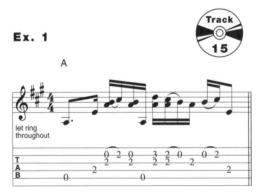

Taylor is a longtime fan of fingerstyle blues guitar. Even though he isn't identified with the style, it's there to be found in his playing. **Example 2**'s setting is a mid-tempo ballad, and a sparkly fill on the upper strings is right in character. But the part here does have the marks of a blues fill, with 6ths sliding up and back, open strings in play against an *E* chord, and a suspension tugging the *E* to and from resolution.

Ex. 2

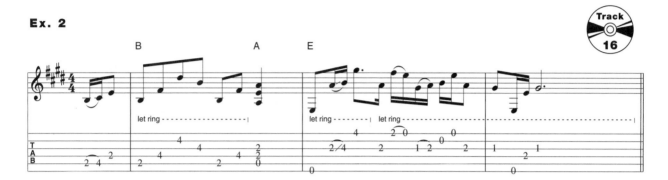

While pretty changes and gentle fills are Taylor's stock in trade, much of his individuality stems from a unique approach to bass lines. Within a fingerpicked part he'll place non-chord tones in root position, suggest one direction with the bass while the changes travel in contrary motion, and spice up a turnaround with a syncopated fill. **Example 3** includes all three techniques, and its bass line alternately complements and counters the arpeggiated changes in a melody of its own.

Ex. 3

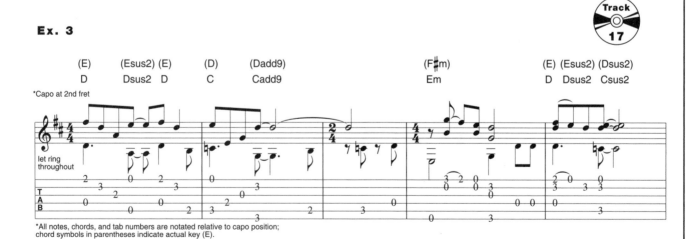

*Capo at 2nd fret

*All notes, chords, and tab numbers are notated relative to capo position;
chord symbols in parentheses indicate actual key (E).

CHAPTER 6 Pete Townshend

▶ Pete Townshend is the quintessential "stealth" acoustic guitarist. Much of the Who's sonic bombast was built on a bed of acoustic guitar, a recording technique that provided shimmering tones to the layered sledgehammer power chords of his Les Paul. Like Keith Richards and the Rolling Stones, Townshend and the Who understood that a good acoustic song could carry itself with or without amplification and overdrive. For Townshend, the bristling electricity of his acoustic playing would prove to be the band's most crucial component.

BIOGRAPHY

Peter Dennis Blandford Townshend was born on May 19, 1945, in Chiswick, England. A rebellious kid from the get-go, Townshend found an outlet in playing the guitar. He put together a number of groups in his teens—even paying his dues on banjo in a Dixieland band—before settling into a band called the Detours with vocalist Roger Daltrey and bassist John Entwistle in 1963. Keith Moon then took over the drum seat, and the band changed its name to the High Numbers before settling on the Who.

A year later, the group was the darling of London's "mod" scene, foppishly dressed teens who relished style over substance. The Who's outlandish and outrageous stage act focused on aural assaults and the destruction of equipment, which mattered more to their mod audience than did the songs. The Who's sheer energy packed the local clubs.

Townshend's earliest songs, including "The Kids Are Alright" and "Magic Bus," were recorded on acoustic guitar. They were short and simple pop songs, written more to express his own angst than to demonstrate virtuoso musicianship. It soon became clear, however, that Moon and Entwistle *were* virtuosos, and Townshend wisely let their instruments define the band's sound. Townshend transferred the band's onstage ferocity to the controlled studio environment by allowing Entwistle and Moon to provide the driving rock elements while he aggressively flailed away on his acoustic.

The band first gained international attention with the release of "I Can See for Miles" in 1967. Coupled with impressive performances at Woodstock and the Monterey Pop Festival, the band finally rose above its club-scene roots. Yet the Who might have been just one more component of the British Invasion had it not been for the release of Townshend's rock opera *Tommy*, in 1969. The band hit its stride with the double album, both conceptually and sonically. From the instrumental "Sparks" to the signature "Pinball Wizard" to "Tommy, Can You Hear Me?" the record was performed as much on acoustic as on electric. Again, the listener experienced much of the band's rock power courtesy of Moon and Entwistle.

CHECKLIST ✓

Guitar . . . . Gibson J-200, Guild JF65-12 12-string, Takamine FP360SC

Setup . . . . Standard

Strings . . . . Ernie Ball medium (.013–.056), Gibson Sonomatics

Pickups . . . . Fishman piezo bridge

Amplification . . . Various, Demeter direct box

Effects . . . . Doubling

Tone . . . . Bright

Picking . . . . Fingerpicking (claw-style, with thumb and first two fingers) and flatpicking

Attack . . . . Ferocious

Signature traits . . . . Staccato strumming, frenetic rhythms

Influences . . . . . . Bob Dylan, Ray Davies, Mose Allison, John Lee Hooker

Overall approach . . . . A belief that the acoustic guitar can rock as heavily as the electric

SELECTED DISCOGRAPHY

With the Who:

The Who Sings My Generation (MCA, 1965)

Happy Jack (Decca, 1967)

The Who Sell Out (Decca, 1967)

Magic Bus (MCA, 1968)

Tommy (MCA, 1969)

Who's Next (MCA, 1971)

Meaty Beaty Big and Bouncy (MCA, 1971)

Quadrophenia (MCA, 1973)

Odds & Sods (MCA, 1974)

The Who by Numbers (MCA, 1975)

Who Are You (1978)

Solo albums:

Who Came First (Rykodisc, 1972)

Empty Glass (Atco, 1980)

RECOMMENDED CUTS

"Bargain" (*Who's Next*)

"Going Mobile" (*Who's Next*)

"Pinball Wizard" (*Tommy*)

"Behind Blue Eyes" (*Who's Next*)

"I'm One" (*Quadrophenia*)

"Dreaming from the Waist" (*Who by Numbers*)

From that point forward, the Who's albums contained masterfully crafted, huge rock songs that showcased Townshend's liberal use of the acoustic guitar and piano. His songwriting and his playing were honed to their finest point with the release of *Who's Next*. The raging rocker "Behind Blue Eyes" opened with a lightly picked acoustic, as did "Going Mobile." Like the best of Townshend's compositions, the delicate opening bars of these songs gave way to rhythmic fury when Pete let the rest of the band into the mix. Even when those gates were thrown open, it was still the acoustic that punctuated the heavy rhythms. With *Who's Next*, Townshend proved that the acoustic—albeit a loud one—could hold its own against the heaviest electric guitar.

The apex of Townshend's ability to mix the mild with the mercurial was 1973's *Quadrophenia*. By applying different instrumentation to each song, he was able to create a set of themes that distinguished the moods of the characters in his opera. "I'm One," "The Punk and the Godfather," and "Love, Reign o'er Me" all created a more varied, though less brutal, Who album, and featured even more acoustic guitar than had *Tommy*.

The rollicking "Squeeze Box" and staccato-strummed "Dreaming from the Waist" from 1975's *Who by Numbers* and "Trick of the Light" and "Music Must Change" from 1978's *Who Are You* showed over and over that Townshend had no shortage of great acoustic-driven ideas. But the band was in the process of coming undone. Moon died of an overdose in 1978, and Townshend wrestled with his own drug addiction. Townshend and Daltrey, never the best of friends, openly brawled with each other.

While the composition of the band changed with the addition of drummer Kenney Jones, Townshend's songwriting style did not. Songs like "Athena" from *It's Hard* proved that he was still an enormously talented writer, but it was clear that the band's heart was not in it anymore.

The Who officially broke up in 1982, and Townshend put out several solo albums, although only *Empty Glass* and his periodic one-man performances showed the genius he was capable of. The Who reunited several times over the next two decades, replacing Kenney Jones with Simon Phillips and Zak Starkey, but new material was not forthcoming. As he got older and more cantankerous, Townshend complained of tinnitus caused by years of roaring from his Hiwatt and Marshall amplifiers. To stem further damage, he took to touring with an acoustic guitar, leaving much of the electric playing to sidemen. Seeing Townshend perform his windmill strums on an acoustic was a bit discombobulating, but the songs suffered not an iota.

In 2002, while the band was mounting yet another farewell tour, John Entwistle died of a cocaine-induced heart attack. Townshend and Daltrey are now the only surviving members of the band. Daltrey prods Townshend to create new Who material, but the likelihood of that diminishes with each passing year. While the future of the Who is in doubt (a perennial question mark since the death of Moon), it is likely that Townshend will continue to perform and record as a solo artist. Regardless of what he does going forward, his odd and furious genius will always be a hallmark of both electric and acoustic rock.

GEAR & SETUP

Despite his penchant for smashing electric guitars, Townshend actually stuck with each of his acoustics for quite a long time. Throughout the 1960s he used Harmony 6- and 12-string acoustics, notably a Harmony Sovereign H-1270 12-string.

Just before recording *Tommy* he bought a sunburst Gibson J-200, which was featured on "Pinball Wizard" and became his main guitar for that album. He also added a 12-string Guild JF65-12 to his collection, phasing out the Harmonys. He has since added other Gibson J-200s.

It's not uncommon for Townshend to go through a dozen guitars at an acoustic performance, probably because he knocks each out of tune in the course of any song. He uses several slim-profile acoustic-electrics, dreadnoughts, and cutaways by Takamine, which he endorsed for a time, and Washburn.

Most of his guitars are equipped with Fishman pickups and strung with Ernie Ball mediums (.013–.056). He always uses heavy picks—usually Manny's.

Live, Townshend usually runs his guitars through a Demeter DI and into the soundboard. In the studio he mics his guitars from above, favoring classic tube microphones. Outside of some slight echo and doubling, they are never subjected to the effects and distortion he abuses his electrics with.

STYLE & TECHNIQUE

Townshend is fundamentally a chord player. He has admitted to not being interested in the kind of lead guitar playing his contemporaries embraced, choosing instead to pelt the guitar with stuttered strums and windmill stabs. He often uses a capo within the first five frets to keep his chord forms simple, sing in a comfortable key, and gain the benefit of open (to the capo) strings.

Townshend uses a wealth of chord variations that distinguish his acoustic guitar playing from that of, say, a Neil Young. In major and minor triads he routinely leaves out the 3rd degree since it tends to produce harmonic clashes when seriously pounded; rather, he prefers to hear multiple octaves of roots and 5ths. Lots of suspended chords and sliding forms (such as taking an open *D* shape up and down the neck) help create Townshend's signature sound. He frequently builds motifs into his songs with alternate voicings up the neck, typically on the upper four or three strings. Against such forms, the droning of open strings—amplified by his frenzied strumming of all six strings—adds harmonic elements that wouldn't be heard with typical voicings or a more restrained strumming technique.

Townshend goes at the guitar with right-hand abandon, not unlike Keith Moon's approach to the drums. Yet Townshend's left hand is rarely very busy, providing a fairly stable element that his strumming and flailing and windmilling can work around.

His playing may get frantic, but it's seldom out of control. On quieter numbers and on those pre-exploded opening verses, a variety of techniques informs his acoustic playing. He adeptly applies each to suit his compositions: flatpicked arpeggios for "Behind Blue Eyes," gently undulating strums for "Love, Reign o'er Me," Travis picking for "I'm One." While long nails aid most guitarists in their fingerpicking, Townshend has said he struggles with the technique since he bites his nails.

To many people's surprise, Townshend has been able to make his Who songs work in intimate solo acoustic performances. This is because, for all the rock-band bombast, the songs never strayed far from the way Townshend conceived them on acoustic. Stripped of bass and drums, many Who albums could have been acoustic gems in their own right.

The "quiet to loud" verse to chorus—which became a cliché after Kurt Cobain employed it in Nirvana (think "Smells Like Teen Spirit")—was perfected much earlier by Townshend. In Townshend's work, quiet and loud parts have always been integrated; the acoustic is not added but intrinsic. The Who's most popular songs open with acoustic chords that explode into thunderous rock when Moon's drums and Entwistle's carpet-bomb bass enter the tune. Townshend likes to accentuate his hardest acoustic blasts with a Spanish-like flourish—a pair of 32nd-notes, like a rolled "r," often preface his power-chord slams.

The band's most famous work, "Pinball Wizard," is distinguished by Townshend's machine-gun strumming of suspended chords, and it follows this same structure. Even in full-on choruses the acoustic is always there, dictating pace and pulse. It is as important as—and in rhythmic counterpoint to—the drums.

Interestingly, Townshend always played his electric as if it were an acoustic. The electric rhythms that power a song like "Won't Get Fooled Again," for instance, are identical to the rhythmic stylings he employs on acoustic in dozens of other selections. Large chords that ring and resonate on an acoustic become pile drivers on an overdriven electric.

LESSON

Townshend is a master of tension and release. **Example 1** contains the tension Townshend frequently builds into an intro. A steady pedal-tone on open *A* builds tension while the changes above it take unexpected turns.

The part does come to resolution, but true release occurs at the top of the next eight-bar section (**Ex. 2**). The bombast of full chords and syncopated parts is completely at odds with the steady pedals that have been established. In such an arrangement, the Who would typically explode here with electric power chords, drums and cymbal crashes, crawling bass lines, maybe a raspy scream—but it's still the acoustic kicking all the instrumental parts into gear.

Ex. 1

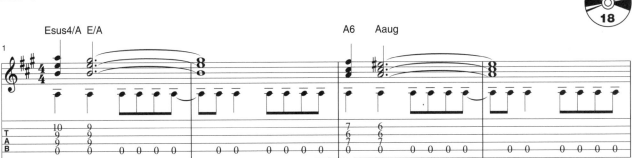

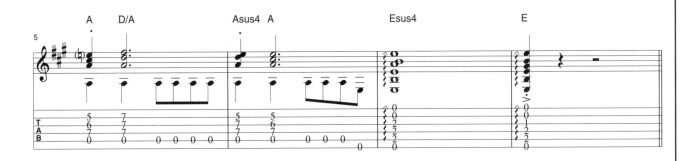

Ex. 2

Track 19

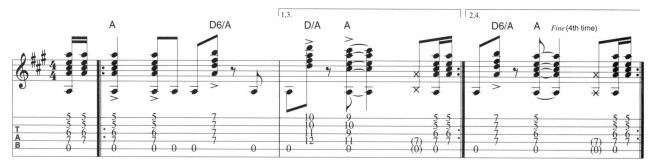

Steady eighth-notes in the bass, alternating from low *G* to open *D*, are the first cue that this is Townshend's take on Travis picking (**Ex. 3**). The movement on the upper strings requires that the low *G* be cemented in place with the *thumb* of the left hand. To stay out of trouble with the picking hand, use only your thumb, 1st, and 2nd fingers; getting your 3rd finger into the mix (it is tempting to grab the *G* on the high string) will mess up your pattern. Note the tricky little harmony for the transition: The chords at work are *D–C/D–Dmin7–C/D*. Even when the lower notes are between the 4th and 3rd strings, as over these *D* bars, keep playing them with your right-hand thumb.

Ex. 3

Track 20

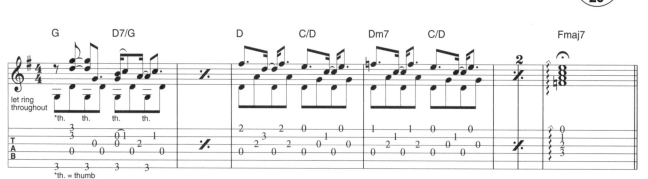

CHAPTER 7 Eagles

(From left) Randy Meisner, Don Henley, Bernie Leadon, and Glenn Frey.

In the wake of the country-folk-rock movement of the late 1960s and '70s, the Eagles emerged to create the modern California sound—an acoustic-based amalgam of the most popular laid-back California bands that had come before, from the Beach Boys to Crosby, Stills, Nash & Young. Underlying the West Coast veneer was a group of serious guitarists who knew how to layer their instruments into a dense yet delicate sound. Always meticulous in their playing and production, the Eagles' integration of three guitars—by three different guitarists—is at the core of their easygoing brand of classic rock.

BIOGRAPHY

The Eagles and their California sound came together by happenstance, a confluence of non-Californians who headed west to record their music. Guitarist Bernie Leadon (born July 19, 1947) was from Minneapolis and was a member of country-rock stalwarts the Flying Burrito Brothers. Guitarist Glenn Frey (November 6, 1948) was from Detroit, where he had worked as a guitarist in Bob Seger's band and had formed a duo with John David (J.D.) Souther. A Nebraska native, bassist Randy Meisner was a founding member of Poco and had worked in Rick Nelson's Stone Canyon Band. Drummer Don Henley was a Texas native who recorded with the band Shiloh.

Each of them had been orbiting the fringe of L.A.'s country-folk-rock scene, which in the early '70s was dominated by David Geffen's Asylum Records and performers like Joni Mitchell, Linda Ronstadt, and Jackson Browne. In 1971 Ronstadt hired Frey and Henley for her backup band and during her summer tour added Leadon and Meisner. However, the four future Eagles played only one gig together with Ronstadt—at Disneyland.

Geffen, who had allegedly signed Frey and Souther to his label as a favor to Jackson Browne, convinced Frey that he should make a real group out of the hired hands in Ronstadt's band. Frey enlisted Henley, Leadon, and Meisner and formed Eagles (technically, there is no "the" in the band's name), crafting songs that fit the SoCal country-folk-rock mold. Unlike his predecessor in CSNY or even the Byrds, each member of the Eagles was an integral part of each song regardless of composer. Frey's acoustic guitar provided the band's underpinning, while Leadon provided country-inflected electric leads and acoustic accompaniment. Meisner and Henley rounded out the band as a rock rhythm section. All of them contributed to the group's vocal harmonies, which had an air of perfection.

The Eagles fused the country sound of artists like Gram Parsons with the acoustic balladry of Browne and CSNY-style vocals to create their 1972 self-titled debut. The two standouts from that album, "Take It Easy" and "Peaceful Easy Feeling," proved to be the prototypes upon which their career would be built: strummed acoustics propelled by a smooth rhythm section and a layer of lead guitar. In the years since, the formula has never failed them.

The band staked out more country-rock territory when they released 1973's *Desperado*. This pseudo–concept album created California outlaw imagery, best remembered on the title track and the acoustically lush "Tequila Sunrise." Though the Eagles included by-the-numbers rock songs on the album, it was the acoustic cuts that most appealed to their growing fan base.

In an attempt to make a harder rock statement, the group brought in another guitarist, Don Felder (born on September 21, 1947). Floridian Felder was a friend of Leadon's and had gigged with Stephen Stills. While he toughened up the band's guitar attack with his versatility, the popular favorite on the next album, 1974's *On the Border*, proved to be yet another acoustic tune. "The Best of My Love" took the band to No. 1 on the music charts.

One of These Nights, released in 1975, stayed true to form. While the title track provided a glimpse at a darker L.A. sound, the band hung its collective hat on yet another pair of acoustic ballads: "Lyin' Eyes" and "Take It to the Limit."

Unhappy with the band's successful rock and pop leanings, Leadon left during the subsequent tour to pursue his country muse, and was replaced by another member of the Asylum stable, Joe Walsh (born in Kansas on November 20, 1947). Known for his exceptional hard-rock work with the James Gang and as an idiosyncratic soloist, Walsh seemed an odd fit for the band. Between Walsh and the Eagles there was little common ground—beyond sharing a label and a manager. Yet his addition worked, as the release of *Hotel California* proved. In this smashingly successful record the Eagles melded a collection of dark acoustic and electric songs that remains the hallmark of the California sound. Their use of three guitars—something more commonly associated with Southern rock bands like the Outlaws—allowed the Eagles to capitalize on each guitarist's approach. Having expanded the band's appeal to arena-rock proportions, *Hotel California* became one of the best-selling albums of all time.

But the band had effectively run its course. Meisner left and was replaced by Timothy B. Schmit (who had, oddly enough, also replaced Meisner in Poco). While Frey and Henley battled for control of the band, the Eagles released *The Long Run* in 1979, an album that was polished to the point of lifelessness. Neither the original country-folk-rock sound that had rung so clearly in the early acoustic releases nor the edge and depth evidenced on *Hotel California* survived the slick production and bland tunes. After its release Henley and Frey recorded successful solo albums, and the band officially threw in the towel in 1982, with Henley vowing to play with the other Eagles only "when hell freezes over."

CHECKLIST ✓

Guitar . . . . Takamine

Setup . . . . Standard

Strings . . . . Ernie Ball

Amplification . . . Trace Elliot TA C200 Acoustic amps; Pendulum preamps

Effects . . . . Minimal, mostly ambient; over-dubbed layers

Tone . . . . Even

Picking . . . . Flatpicked

Attack . . . . Steady, strummed with elbow as fulcrum

Signature traits . . . . Open-position strums; orchestrated; melding styles of different guitarists

Influences . . . . . . CSNY, the Byrds, Jackson Browne, Gram Parsons

Overall approach . . . . Laid-back, conservative

SELECTED DISCOGRAPHY

Eagles (Asylum, 1972)
Desperado (Asylum, 1973)
On the Border (Asylum, 1974)
One of These Nights (Asylum, 1975)
Their Greatest Hits 1971–1975
   (Asylum, 1976)
Hotel California (Asylum, 1976)
The Long Run (Asylum, 1979)
Eagles Live (Asylum, 1980)
Hell Freezes Over (Geffen, 1994).

RECOMMENDED CUTS
(Most available on *Their Greatest Hits 1971–1975*)
"Hotel California" (*Hotel California*)
"Best of My Love" (*On the Border*)
"Take It Easy" (*Eagles*)
"Tequila Sunrise" (*Desperado*)
"Lyin' Eyes" (*One of These Nights*)

The allure of millions of dollars proved to be more persuasive than the temperature in Hades, and the band reunited for an "MTV Unplugged" show, followed by a live album and several immensely successful and immensely profitable tours. During this time, even Henley demonstrated his guitar ability night after night. Felder was fired in 2001 (ostensibly over a share of the band's profits) and proceeded to sue his former bandmates. In 2003 the remaining Eagles—Frey, Walsh, Henley, and Schmit—began recording the Eagles' first studio album in more than 20 years and prepare for the "Farewell 1" Tour.

In retrospect, the Eagles managed to attract a wider audience than most of their SoCal contemporaries—including respected singer-songwriters like Neil Young and James Taylor—by bringing their soft acoustic sounds into the context of a rock band. Their appeal crossed genres and age groups, ranging from easy listening to straight-ahead rock, from teens to adults. Today, when one says "classic rock," the Eagles are held up as the standard-bearers of that term—not too hard, not too soft, and able to fit into any radio playlist. The band's legacy may be tarnished by their economically inspired reunions, but there is no denying that at their acoustic best, the Eagles produced some of the genre's most distinctive work.

GEAR & SETUP

Despite having a contingent of three guitarists in the band at any one time (four, if we include Henley), the gear choices of the individual Eagles are surprisingly similar. The band has a long-term endorsement deal with Takamine, so Takamine 6- and 12-strings predominate on record and in concert. Frey and Henley use them exclusively. Walsh, for his part, is known as one of the most avid guitar collectors in the world, having owned hundreds of rare and vintage instruments. With the Eagles, he adds a

Gibson J-200 to his Takamine collection. Felder also used a Gibson J-200. Ernie Ball strings are used on the vast majority of the guitars.

Trace Elliot Acoustic amps are the band's standard (usually the TA C200 Acoustic Combo), coupled with Pendulum preamps. Much of Walsh's rig is custom designed.

The band uses an array of effects for its electric work, yet keeps its acoustics relatively effects-free. The only effects are minimal chorus, delay, and layer upon layer of doubling in the studio.

STYLE & TECHNIQUE

Since the Eagles were composed of guitarists with markedly different styles, the band had no single identifiable technique. In fact, it is the seamless integration of each player's style into every Eagles cut that defined its sound. The classic Eagles arrangement includes a foundation of strummed acoustics; steady rhythms attacked with a light pick establish the song's feel and set the tempo as effectively as a drummer's hi-hat. Fills, played on electric, weave in and out of early verses and choruses. The arrangement grows as the song progresses, often peaking (in guitar terms) at a solo that incorporates dual guitars playing in counterpoint or in harmony.

If any single member's style is most emblematic of their acoustic approach, it is Glenn Frey's. His steady rhythms, honed from his rock playing with Bob Seger, translated easily to acoustic guitar and provided the bed for much of the Eagles' music. Frey's natural rhythms, often executed with simple chords in open position, account for the band's accessibility to both listener and player. Frey occasionally uses open tunings, such as open *E* on "Heartache Tonight."

During his time with the band Leadon added a light electric touch that was more country than rock. More than any of the other guitarists, he was responsible for the band's early country-rock leanings. Felder, at the time of his hiring, was a more accomplished guitarist than his compatriots. His role was akin to that of a session musician, which was the role he had when he first recorded with the group. He had a relatively light and more polished delivery, often adding fills and solo touches. Walsh was something of a wild card in the mix, as his style encompassed hard rock riffing, boozy and unpredictable leads, and influences ranging from rockabilly to country to funky rock. Interestingly, Walsh's slide work enhanced the country sound that the band had built with Leadon.

LESSON

It was bands like the Eagles, CSNY, and America that sold a lot of 12-strings in the '70s. The sweet fullness made the most of simple, pretty changes like those found in **Ex. 1**. The strum is basic as well, in steady eighths, but be sure to play the accents shown on beat *one* and on the upbeats of *two* and *three*. The measure of 6ths (bar 8) combined with the open 3rd string enjoys a more complex harmony thanks to the 12-string. When they descend from position VII to open position, they land in the first chord shape of the example.

Ex. 1

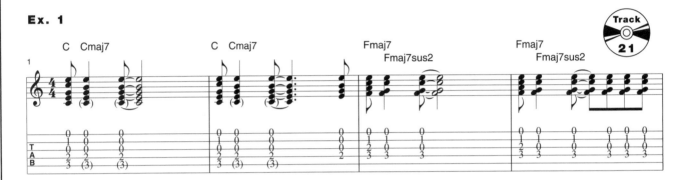

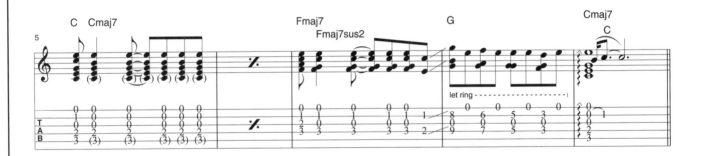

The left-hand part in **Ex. 2** is easy enough, with just a bit of movement around familiar *G* and *C* shapes. It's the strumming hand's rhythm that's harder to present with the busy but subtle delivery required. Your first two strums in the pattern should both be downstrokes. Be careful, though, not to put an accent on that second downstroke, which falls on the first 16th-note. Though all of the feel is generated by the 16th-notes, the accents here fall specifically on beats *one, three,* and *four*. This is a classic country rhythm, recalling the clip-clopping of a horse's step, much as a typical maraca rhythm does.

Ex. 2

Track 22

With the band having at least two capable lead players, Eagles solos are by and large performed on electric guitars. However, occasional acoustic-only settings reveal that their leads hold up well in more sparse surroundings. In **Ex. 3** a Spanish-style lick leads into chord-based arpeggios. The pull-off in the first measure is shown in 16ths, but should be delivered as an ornamentation. The first measure's lick ends on the same note (*F#*) that starts the *Bm* arpeggio in the next bar, so be sure to clearly articulate the note both times. The chords outlined by the lead's arpeggios—*Bm* and *F#7*—are heard on a 12-string over the second measure.

Track 23

Ex. 3

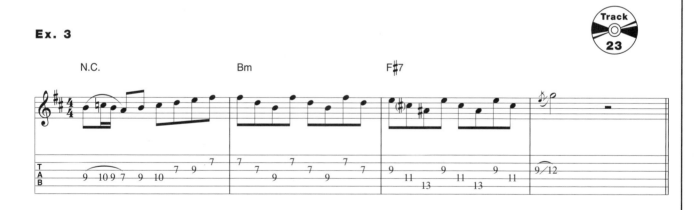

CHAPTER 8 Tom Petty

Despite his early rock success with the Heartbreakers, Tom Petty has proven to be a dyed-in-the-wool country folk-rocker with an appreciation for the kind of acoustic guitar playing embodied by musicians such as Neil Young and Bob Dylan. During the late 1980s, in defiance of conventional wisdom, Petty was the only mainstream rocker indulging a taste for acoustic guitar. Not only was it unexpected, but Petty's acoustic preference led to his greatest commercial success.

BIOGRAPHY

Born on October 20, 1950, in Gainesville, Florida, Thomas Earl Petty began playing guitar in high school, influenced in great part by the country folk-rock coming out of Southern California. This included everyone from the Byrds to Buffalo Springfield, with a liberal dose of Bob Dylan thrown in.

As an aspiring guitarist, Petty dropped out of the University of Florida to join Mudcrutch, a band that contained the seeds of what would one day become the Heartbreakers. Petty and the band moved to L.A. in search of a record contract and were signed to Shelter in 1970. However, Mudcrutch disintegrated before it could release an album, and Petty was given a solo deal by Shelter. Instead of going it alone, though, he tried his luck unsuccessfully with a handful of forgettable SoCal bands.

In 1975 Petty reconnected with a couple of members of Mudcrutch—guitarist Mike Campbell and keyboard player Benmont Tench—who had since teamed up with bassist Ron Blair and drummer Stan Lynch. Called the Heartbreakers, the new band played a uniquely American mix of Byrds-style jangly folk-rock and gritty garage-band rock. In 1976 Petty, as their lead singer, brought the band back to Shelter as part of his solo deal. *Tom Petty & the Heartbreakers* was released in the U.S.—and completely ignored. Undaunted, the band headed to Europe, where constant touring won them a large British following. Taking another stab at the U.S. market, Shelter released the slinky "Breakdown" along with "American Girl." This time, radio stations paid attention.

The singles paved the way for *You're Gonna Get It*, another slice of SoCal garage rock. Just as Petty looked ready for the big time, Shelter was absorbed by MCA, which refused to renegotiate Petty's original deal. Instead of living with the existing deal, Petty declared bankruptcy in 1979. MCA capitulated to Petty's demands, and the band released its breakthrough, *Damn the Torpedoes*. Sounding like the work of an amphetamine-fueled Byrds—complete with Rickenbacker guitars and Dylanesque vocals—the record contained several hits, along with the acoustic "Louisiana Rain," a portent of Petty's future acoustic work.

CHECKLIST ✓

Guitar . . . . Martin, Gibson acoustics

Strings . . . . SIT, Martin Marquis

Pickups . . . . L.R. Baggs, Fishman

Amplification . . . Avalon DIs

Tone . . . . Crisp, full

Attack . . . . Measured and moderate

Signature
traits . . . . Classic country-rock figures and tone

Influences . . . . . . The Byrds, Bob Dylan

Overall
approach . . . . Song-based, lucid

SELECTED DISCOGRAPHY

Tom Petty & the Heartbreakers
(Warner Bros., 1976)
Damn the Torpedoes (MCA, 1979)
Hard Promises (MCA, 1981)
Long After Dark (MCA, 1982)
Southern Accents (MCA, 1985)
The Traveling Wilburys, Vol. 1
(Wilbury, 1988)
Full Moon Fever (MCA, 1989)
Into the Great Wide Open (MCA, 1991)
Wildflowers (Warner Bros., 1994)
Echo (Warner Bros., 1999)

RECOMMENDED CUTS

"Free Fallin'" *(Full Moon Fever)*
"Alright for Now" *(Full Moon Fever)*
"Louisiana Rain" *(Damn the Torpedoes)*
"Into the Great Wide Open"
(*Into the Great Wide Open*)
"It'll All Work Out" (*Let Me Up [I've Had Enough]; 1987, MCA*)
"A Face in the Crowd" (*Full Moon Fever*)

Despite ongoing record company hassles, the band released a slew of pop albums in 1980s, including *Hard Promises*, *Southern Accents*, and *Let Me Up (I've Had Enough)*. Following Petty's patented SoCal garage rock sound, all offered up hit after hit. At the same time, the various members of the Heartbreakers—stellar musicians in their own right—became notable session men for other California rockers, from Don Henley to Stevie Nicks. Their notoriety assured, Petty and the Heartbreakers were hired to back up Dylan on his 1986 tour.

The relationship with Dylan led to the formation of the Traveling Wilburys, a folk-rock "supergroup" featuring Petty and Dylan, George Harrison, Roy Orbison, and Jeff Lynne of the Electric Light Orchestra. Petty contributed "Last Night" to the Wilburys' debut album, an acoustic country-rock tune that would serve as a template for a good portion of his subsequent work. Petty also had a string of personal crises, from breaking his hand to having his house burn down.

Petty released his first solo album, *Full Moon Fever*, in 1989. The most successful of his career, the album was equal parts country folk-rock and rockabilly, leaving Petty's harder rock inclinations behind. It opened with "Free Fallin'," a 6-string ode to all things Los Angeles (good and bad—with Petty it can be difficult to discern sarcasm). The album also included the haunting acoustic jangle and slide of "A Face in the Crowd" along with "Alright for Now," a piece that could have come from David Crosby's acoustic songbook.

Petty reunited with the Heartbreakers for several more albums (and the Wilburys for one more) before releasing his second solo record, *Wildflowers*. Another country-imbued effort, it featured the title track, the simplistic "You Don't Know How It Feels" (combining everything Petty had learned from Dylan and Young) and "Don't Fade on Me," an acoustic fingerpicking duet with Mike Campbell.

Petty continued in the same vein with *Echo* in 1999 and *The Last DJ* in 2002, as well as music for the soundtrack to the film *She's the One.* In 2003 Petty enlisted Scott Thurston as the band's third guitarist. This addition allowed the group to recreate elements in performance that would otherwise be lost between studio and stage.

Having been at it for nearly 25 years, Petty and the Heartbreakers continue to tour and record. Petty, for his part, has settled into a comfortable role as one of the elder statesmen of American rock 'n' roll.

GEAR & SETUP

Petty and Campbell are both avid guitar collectors, but they rely on a handful of mainstays. Petty's onstage favorites include two Gibsons: a '95 Everly Bros. J-185 (equipped with an L.R. Baggs Saddle Transducer pickup), and a '95 J-200. Both are strung with SIT Royal Bronze strings (.012–.054) and sent through Avalon DIs. His 12-string of choice is a 1978 Guild D212-M—which actually belongs to Campbell. It's strung with light-gauge Ernie Ball Earthwood strings and has a Fishman Active Matrix pickup sent through an Avalon DI.

In the studio Petty frequently uses a 1964 Gibson Hummingbird (with Martin Marquis light strings), a '73 Martin 12-28 12-string (Ernie Ball Earthwood lights), and a '77 Martin D-41 (Martin Marquis lights).

Martin is currently developing matching 6- and 12-string Tom Petty Signature Editions, due to be unveiled in 2004. The dreadnought bodies will be constructed with Italian Alpine spruce soundboards and East Indian rosewood back and sides, and will include active onboard electronics. On the fingerboard, an inlayed moon-and-stars motif will evoke the artwork from *Full Moon Fever.* The instruments' ornamentation will blend attributes of Martin's 28 and 45 styles.

Onstage Campbell primarily plays a 1993 Takamine Koa PT-406, strung with SIT Royal Bronze strings (.012–.054) and sent through an Avalon DI. Five well-aged acoustics have appeared on his recorded tracks time and again: a 1950 Martin 00-18, an early '70s D-28 (both strung with Martin Marquis lights), a '78 Guild D212-M (the same 12-string Petty loves), a Guild F-50, and a '78 Ovation for Nashville tuning.

Scott Thurston plays a 2002 Gibson ADV Jumbo, a '71 Martin D-18, and a 1935 Gibson L-00. All are strung with SIT Royal Bronze sets, .012–.054.

In the studio, guitars are miked with Sennheiser 451 and 69 mics as well as Neumann 47 tube mics.

STYLE & TECHNIQUE

Petty's acoustic technique, in keeping with his general approach, is elemental and organic. No point overanalyzing or ascribing complexity where there is none—he has a documented interest in representing his songs with time-tested changes and forms. Simplicity in and of itself, though, would be worthless without taste. Petty's tact and individuality are revealed in his crafting of hooks, his arrangements of parts, and his ability to write a melody against those parts that is both unexpected and accessible.

His playing style lies right between that of George Harrison and Neil Young. On the one hand, he shares the same country and rockabilly inclinations that Harrison had, and he plays guitar parts that serve first and foremost to support the song and the vocals. But like Young, he is able to create distinctive phrases from his use of simple chords and accented strumming. Nowhere is this better exemplified than in "Free Fallin'," where the entire song is summed up in the opening changes: simple and simply strummed chords. He appreciates the value of big, chiming chords that can stand on their own. His recordings are a hybrid of the jangly Byrds sound, which featured strumming and arpeggios, and the bigger sustained and open sound of Townshend.

Petty's songs and guitar work benefit enormously from Mike Campbell's contributions. Beyond his electric leads, which can vary from squonky slide to gentle, full-toned lines, Campbell weaves precise arpeggios, melodies, and alternate-voiced parts into Petty's song-based strumming. Between the two of them, a basic *C–D–G* progression can yield a complete orchestration. Campbell also adds acoustic touches with bouzouki, mandolin, and dulcimer.

Petty songs are available to the novice who wants to knock out a simple tune, while providing healthy reminders to the seasoned player about good composition and arranging.

LESSON

A popular technique for achieving a rich, deep acoustic sound within a song is to stack similar parts one on top of the next. With capos, 12-strings, and Nashville-tuned guitars, a simple progression can take on grand proportions as the voices multiply. Throughout **Ex. 1**'s progression, no more than three notes are heard at any one time—but they're heard in multiple octaves and, in the second example, on two guitars. The first part is a 12-string, strumming the changes in open position.

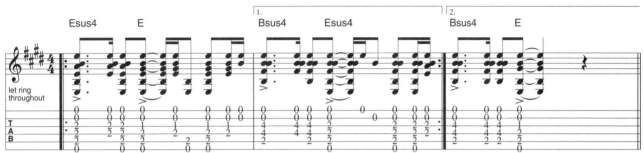

Now the 6-string is added (**Ex. 2**). With the exception of a single note (there's no D#—written in the capoed example as C#—in the 12-string's *Bsus4* chord), the second part plays the same chords in a new voicing. Capo at the 2nd fret and start on a *Dsus4* shape; with the capo, it sounds *Esus4*, just as in the 12-string's part. The rest of the progression follows suit, with familiar first-string suspensions and an open *A* shape. Combined, the 12-string and capoed 6-string build a wall of guitars.

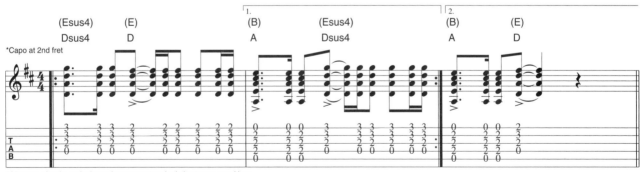

*All notes, chords, and tab numbers are notated relative to capo position; chord symbols in parentheses indicate actual key (E).

Example 3 also combines capoed and open guitars, but with very distinct approaches on each. In the open part (heard in the right channel) a low-key line is plucked on the 4th and 3rd strings of a *D* chord, with the notes *D* and *F♯* remaining planted on the top two strings. For the higher-voiced arpeggio part (left channel), capo at the 7th fret. (Note: It's wise to check your tuning whenever capoing, since the capo's stop usually makes wound strings go sharp.) The chords played high up on the neck—*D* and *Asus4*—are played in a fixed fingerpicking pattern. Play their 16ths in even rhythm, allowing every note to ring as you pick.

Ex. 3

Track 26

*Gtr. 2 notes and tab positions are notated relative to capo; actual key (D).

Another popular Petty approach is heard in **Ex. 4**, an upbeat strumming pattern with a moving lower line. Capo at the 5th fret and use a medium-gauge pick: strong enough to pluck out the main line, but flexible enough to emphasize the bouncing 16th-note rhythm with percussive attacks. Keep your 1st and 4th fingers in position while your 2nd and 3rd manage the notes—many of them hammered—that work like a bass line.

Ex. 4

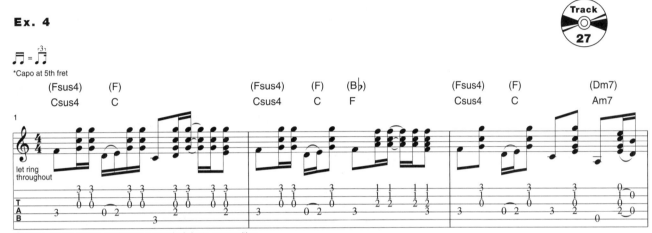

*Capo at 5th fret

*All notes, chords, and tab numbers are notated relative to capo position; chord symbols in parentheses indicate actual key (F).

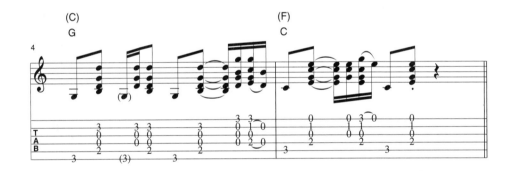

CHAPTER 9 Peter Buck

R.E.M. forged the alternative movement of the 1980s with an eclectic blend of folk instrumentation, backwoods simplicity, and indecipherable lyrics. While the band's minimalist approach was an unlikely recipe for success in any genre, Peter Buck's uncomplicated playing, which relied on layers of strummed and arpeggiated chords, paved the way for guitarists that couldn't—or wouldn't—plaster gymnastic solos over everything they recorded. Incorporating a wide array of acoustic instruments, from guitar and piano to mandolin and banjo, R.E.M. and Peter Buck turned the raw strumming of the guitar into a dominant physical form from the mid-1980s on to the new millennium.

BIOGRAPHY

Peter Buck was born on December 6, 1956, in Oakland, California, but his family moved in fits and starts across the country, from San Francisco to Indiana and finally to Roswell, Georgia. Inspired by all things pop, Buck listened to big-name acts like the Beatles, the Byrds, and the Rolling Stones, while indulging his passion for obscure players by poring over album racks and music magazines.

He bought his first guitar at age 17 for $55, learning chords and songs from his older brother. Instead of going to college, he hitchhiked around the United States for a few years before returning to Georgia in 1978 and settling in the college town of Athens. With his extensive knowledge of music, Buck got a job working at Wuxtry's, a local record store frequented by another fan of eclectic music, Michael Stipe.

With a shared musical interest, Buck and Stipe became friends. Together they joined a local rock band that included drummer Bill Berry. In 1980 Buck, Berry, and Stipe decided to form their own band, adding Berry's friend Mike Mills on bass. After performing under the name Twisted Kites, the band settled on R.E.M. (for "rapid eye movement") as their official moniker.

R.E.M.'s earliest music was built on simple folk-song structures of the type popular in and around the Appalachians, often utilizing little more than strummed minor chords

CHECKLIST ✓

Guitar . . . . Taylor cutaway 615

Setup . . . . High-strung, jumbo frets

Strings . . . . Dean Markley heavy: .013, .017, .026, .036, .046, .056

Pickups . . . . Sunrise Electronics

Amplification . . . Avalon U5 DI (Class A), Sunrise preamp

Effects . . . . None

Tone . . . . Natural

Picking . . . . . Flatpicks with custom-made Jim Dunlop 73mms

Attack . . . . Heavy-handed, occasionally frenetic

Signature traits . . . . Arpeggiated chords; tinkling mandolins and dulcimers against strummed acoustics

Influences . . . . . . The Who, Neil Young, the Velvet Underground

Overall approach . . . . Folk-based

SELECTED DISCOGRAPHY

Chronic Town EP (IRS, 1982)
Murmur (A&M, 1983)
Reckoning (A&M, 1984)
Fables of the Reconstruction
    (MCA, 1985)
Life's Rich Pageant (MCA, 1986)
Document (MCA, 1987)
Out of Time (Warner Bros., 1991)
Automatic for the People
    (Warner Bros., 1992)

RECOMMENDED CUTS

"Talk About the Passion" (*Murmur*)
"Perfect Circle" (*Murmur*)
"Driver 8" (*Fables of the
    Reconstruction*)
"(Don't Go Back to) Rockville"
    (*Reckoning*)
"Fall on Me" (*Life's Rich Pageant*)
"Flowers of Guatemala" (*Life's Rich
    Pageant*)
"Me in Honey" (*Out of Time*)
"Losing My Religion" (*Out of Time*)
"Man on the Moon" (*Automatic for the
    People*)
"Endgame" (*Out of Time*)
"Find the River" (*Automatic for the
    People*)

in open position. Stipe's enigmatic lyrics and mumbled vocals created a seemingly dark and complex element to the band. Buck, playing the band's primary instrument, responded by adding more complex structures to his guitar playing. Feeling that he wasn't a proficient guitarist, Buck made the most of the chords in his repertoire, dressing them up with arpeggios, suspensions, and active bass lines. Combined with straight-up rock rhythms on the bass and drums, the result was a haunting quasi-folk-rock sound with an unschooled aggressiveness and a "throw it out there" garage-band primitiveness. But R.E.M. did it with an appreciation of pop, counting on melody and organic rhythms at a time when dance music and synth-drenched New Wave was dominating the charts.

R.E.M. exhaustively toured the U.S. college circuit, building a rabid following and getting rave reviews from critics. Their live shows were a mixture of energy and raw musicianship, coupled with the regional feel of a hoo-tenanny. They signed to IRS Records via a long-established relationship with the label's owner, Miles Copeland (brother of Police drummer Stewart Copeland). Miles had been in a short-lived punk band with Mills and Berry before those two met up with Buck and Stipe, and he signed his old friends to his label.

The EP *Chronic Town* introduced R.E.M. as a cryptic guitar-pop band with an appreciation for minor keys and engaging hooks. Their first full-length record, 1983's *Murmur*, allowed them to do in the studio what they couldn't do live. With multiple tracks available, they took their simply constructed songs and added layer upon layer of guitars to create a dense atmosphere, as evidenced on tracks like "Talk About the Passion." Buck has claimed that some tracks had as many as 20 layers of guitar, many playing the same part. On record, the music was no longer purely acoustic or folk, but not quite heavy enough to be punk or hard rock.

For *Reckoning*, their second album, the band dispensed with the overdubs, instead choosing to play their compositions as they did live. Relying on acoustic guitars and a Rickenbacker electric (which had the most acoustic sound of any popular electric), Buck continued to build tracks with overdubbed guitars, weaving an increasing number of guitar parts into the arrangements. Still leaning heavily on minor-key harmonies, R.E.M. veered into harder electric sounds with *Fables of the Reconstruction*, a collection of songs linked more by the lyrics' political statements than musical cohesion. The song "Driver 8," a quintessential Buck composition with its electric riff and Byrds-like acoustic chorus, made it to national radio. Listeners above the underground began to take notice.

Life's Rich Pageant exhibited a fuller, more textured sound that better reflected the band's musicianship, and demonstrated more optimism and aggressiveness. Notable was "Fall on Me," which showed Buck's unique ability to make an electric guitar serve as the backdrop for an acoustic. The next album, 1987's *Document*, was a pivotal point for the band both artistically and commercially. The expanded orchestrations included mandolins, bouzoukis, and sitars, and Scott Litt's production lent the clarity missing from earlier releases. The record yielded big hits with "The One I Love" and "It's the End of the World as We Know It . . . ," pushing the band squarely into the mainstream and heralding commercial music's shift away from the hard rock of the mid 1980s.

Suddenly, everyone was looking at R.E.M. as the Next Big Thing. A bidding war among the major labels resulted in the band's signing with Warner Bros., which released *Green* in 1988. If *Document* represented a turning point, *Green* found them all the way around the bend. It was a full-on pop album, featuring electric guitars, effects, and a polished sheen that had longtime fans crying foul. Nonetheless, the album was a huge success, and songs like "Orange Crush" and "Stand" became radio staples. By this time, Buck and R.E.M. hadn't just joined the mainstream—they were the mainstream.

The band went into a two-year seclusion before releasing 1991's *Out of Time*, which included the eerie acoustic numbers "Endgame," "Me in Honey," and the mandolin single "Losing My Religion." The following year R.E.M. produced *Automatic for the People*, a landmark in its catalog that effortlessly blended the best elements of the group's earliest and latest sounds. Strongly produced and painstakingly arranged—John Paul Jones orchestrated the strings—the record featured rock songs in an acoustic context, from the fingerpicked hit "Drive" to the countrified "Man on the Moon."

The band tossed the acoustics overboard for its next two records, the electrically feral *Monster* and *New Adventures in Hi-Fi* (the latter recorded primarily during sound-checks on tour). In a series of almost tragicomic coincidences, Stipe, Mills, and Berry experienced serious individual medical conditions (emergency surgeries, brain aneurysms, tumors) that almost killed the band, literally. After recovering from his illness, and tired from years on the road, Bill Berry bowed out of the group in 1997. The band members' health problems no doubt stopped a few hearts in the Warner Bros. boardroom: Prior to *New Adventures*, the label signed the band to an $80 million, five-album deal, the largest record advance in history.

Subsequent R.E.M. releases *Up* and *Reveal* were substantially less interesting than their predecessors as the remaining three members brought in drum machines and session musicians and toyed with electronic music. Still, fans and critics praised their experimental spirit and reluctance to rest on their laurels.

Buck took to producing indie bands in Seattle and working on side projects, including Tuatara and an album with Mark Eitzel. Outside of R.E.M. he got the most notoriety for an alleged air-rage episode on a flight to London that made him a darling of the British tabloid press. (He was eventually cleared.)

While R.E.M. continues to produce new music, Buck and company can rest comfortably knowing that they almost singlehandedly ushered in an era of alternative music that, if nothing else, killed disco and New Wave.

GEAR & SETUP

Peter Buck's guitar setup is succinctly captured by his personal mantra: "Heavy strings, high frets, and high action equal good tone." He starts with a Taylor cutaway 615 outfitted with jumbo frets and strung with heavy Dean Markleys, .013–056. He sets the strings almost as high as they'll go without losing intonation, about as high as slide players set their strings.

When he records, Peter always uses external mics for his acoustic, positioning a tube mic about ten to eleven inches away from the soundhole. Depending on the tune, he may add a condenser or ribbon mic and mix the signals with the tube mic. He never uses pickups for acoustic recording.

The setup is different live. Buck employs Sunrise Electronics pickups, which detect vibrations from the guitar's top. These run out through an Avalon U5 DI. For smaller venues he'll take the under-saddle transducer pickup built into his Taylor, run it out to a Sunrise preamp, and mix that with the Sunrise pickup signal.

His preamp and amp tone settings are flat. He always runs his guitars dry; effects are added in the studio or on the house system when playing live. That way, his initial guitar signal is as pure as possible, providing a clean sound that can be modified according to the needs of the track or venue.

Buck uses Jim Dunlop 73mm picks, which are no longer available commercially—he pays for custom runs in order to ensure a regular supply.

STYLE & TECHNIQUE

For a straightforward and ostensibly simplistic guitarist, Buck's influences are encyclopedic. Ask him which player inspired a part and he's just as likely to mention Neil Young or Gram Parsons as Steve Cropper, Jimmy Page, Hubert Sumlin, or T-Bone Walker. Likewise, the band has tipped its collective hat to an array of folk, punk, classic-rock, and pop artists, such as the Zombies, the Velvet Underground, the Who, the Troggs (whom Buck backed up on a 1992 comeback attempt), Big Star, and Fleetwood Mac. Because the band members often swap instruments, these sources all find their way into R.E.M. songs.

While Buck draws on many influences, he distills another player's approach rather than copping anyone's technique. His playing shows little trace of mainstream rock; he rarely plays solos in the tradition of rock lead guitarists, his chord changes are far removed from blues forms, and he even plays the electric guitar like an acoustic. Frequent comparisons to Roger McGuinn of the Byrds are spurious; the two share style and instrumentation, not a collection of riffs.

Buck's playing has evolved over the years, with early signatures evident only in passing on post-*Document* tracks. R.E.M. records from the '80s are marked by his arpeggiated chords, the chimey sound referred to as "jangle" guitar. With pick in hand, Buck plucks individual notes of open-position chords, letting one note ring over the next as the picking pattern cycles. Movement within the chords—suspensions, pull-offs, hammers, moving bass lines—lends momentum. His arpeggios often come in rotations: a short pattern of notes is repeated within a few bars, and every time the pattern comes back around, accents fall on different beats.

Another favorite move of Buck's is to shift a line up and down one string while catching an adjacent open string on the attacks, resulting in a simultaneous melody and pedal. In addition to just plain sounding cool, it allows him to establish melodies and hooks without completely sacrificing a rhythm part. Good examples are heard in "Green Grow the Rushes" (*Fables of the Reconstruction*) and "Disturbance at the Heron House" (*Document*).

Even when electrics are in the foreground, R.E.M.'s most characteristic songs rely heavily on a foundation of strummed acoustics (typically played by Buck, though often by Mills or touring member Peter Holsapple). It's in these bedrock parts that the band's folk roots are laid bare: simple chord forms are fully strummed in natural, arm-swinging rhythms.

Unlike Pete Townshend or Keith Richards, both of whom applied electric motifs to the acoustic, Buck has always been first and foremost an acoustic player. More precisely, he's an acoustic player steeped in regional American music. This shows in R.E.M.'s instrumentation, which has frequently integrated instruments considered to be emblematic of the American South, such as mandolin and banjo. Buck's use of these instruments, plus sitar and dulcimer, increased throughout the '90s as the band took increasing care orchestrating their songs. This is exemplified in "Losing My Religion," where the sparse mandolin-against-acoustic figure that introduces the song and provides the hook is gradually enveloped in a rich and complex arrangement.

LESSON

For a sound like the one represented in **Ex. 1**, Buck will often track 12- and 6-string guitars in unison or nearly unison parts. At this slow tempo, and in the key of *Am*, the unisons establish a full but airy background over which to lay vocals. The part pivots entirely on the bass notes; once they're hitting the quarter-notes of the 3/4 rhythm part, the eighth-note strums naturally fill in the gaps. The 12-string is panned toward the left; the 6-string enters in bar 5 and toward the right channel.

Ex. 1

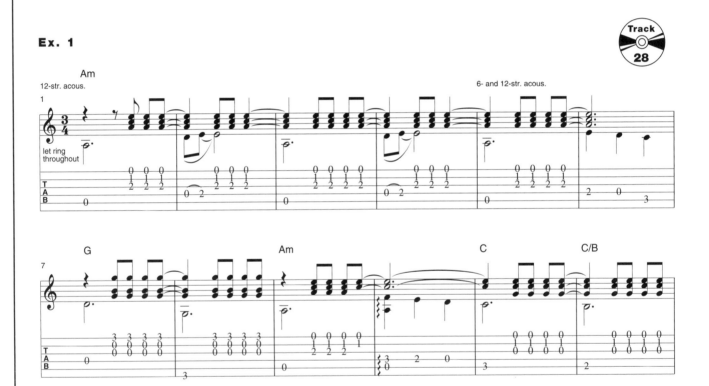

Ex. 1 cont.

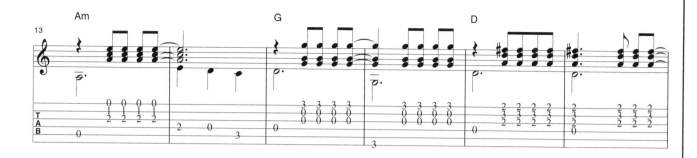

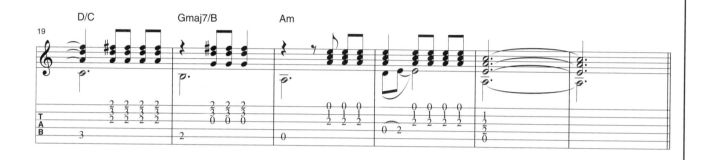

Confirming the folk-based roots of his playing, Buck has featured mandolin and bouzouki parts in the band's pop and rock songs. With the help of a capo, we can emulate the mandolin parts even without retuning to the intervals of the mandolin's open strings (tuned in 5ths: low to high, *GDAE*). In the two parts in **Ex. 2**, the upper staff (Guitar 1) emulates mandolin, while the lower staff (Guitar 2) is a standard 6-string acoustic. For Guitar 1, pick the strings *sul ponticello*—right up against the bridge—to imitate the taut, narrow tone of a mandolin.

Notice the unison *C*'s in Guitar 1's first full measure, mimicking the paired unison strings of a mandolin. Watch the stretch when the 3rd string catches the *E* (written as G♯) over *Am*. Guitar 2 is a basic strum, hammering from open to closed on the third beat of each measure. Doing so on both chord changes gives the part more movement and lends rhythmic counterpoint against Guitar 1.

Ex. 2

Gtr.1 (mandolin arr. for gtr.)
*Capo at 8th fret   N.C.

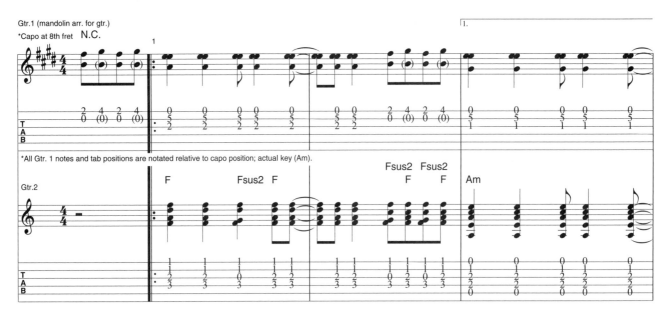

*All Gtr. 1 notes and tab positions are notated relative to capo position; actual key (Am).

Gtr.2

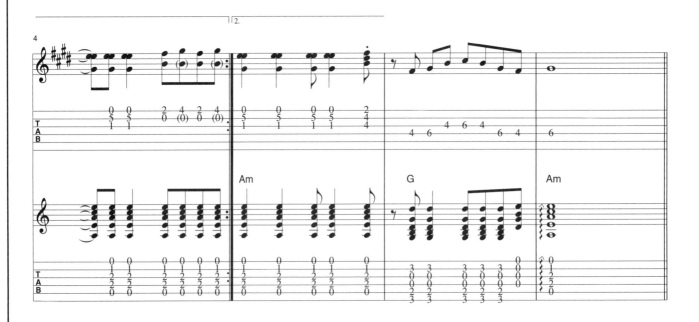

Playing the only polyphonic instrument in the band, Buck is required to fill a lot of space with his guitar. Drone strings and arpeggios are both great ways to deliver a melodic line without having the bottom drop out of an arrangement. A simple but effective two-note riff opens **Ex. 3**, with the open *D* string ringing below. The *D* remains as a foundation as a melodic line rides high on the adjacent 3rd string. Then the opening riff is repeated, this time leading to the chordal arpeggios that resolve the part.

Ex. 3

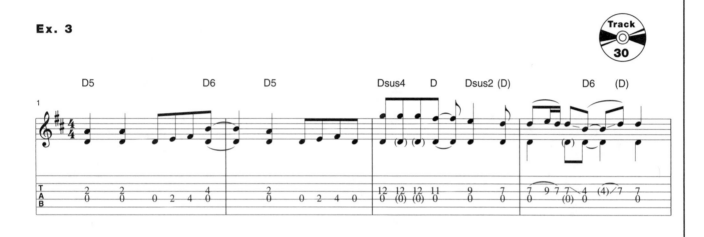

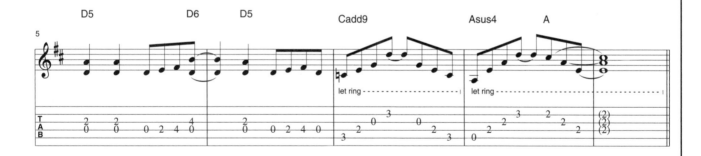

CHAPTER 10 Dave Matthews

▶ Dave Matthews created a successful rock band by not relying on traditional rock elements. The instrumental centerpiece of the Dave Matthews Band is his acoustic guitar, surrounded by horns, violins, jazz-inflected bass lines, and frequently changing tempos. That Matthews could take an acoustic jam band to the top of the commercial music business in the post-grunge era is a testament to his unique songwriting skills and his understanding of the appeal of an unadorned acoustic guitar.

BIOGRAPHY

Dave Matthews was born on January 9, 1967, in Johannesburg, South Africa. He had an early obsession with the Beatles, notably the layered sound and production of *Magical Mystery Tour*. After graduating from high school and facing the possibility of getting drafted for military duty, Matthews moved with his mother to Charlottesville, Virginia. As a guitarist he had varied interests, from the complex chord voicings and time changes of King Crimson's Robert Fripp and Adrian Belew to the ethnic rhythms explored by Paul Simon.

During the late 1980s Matthews worked as a bartender while making home demos of his acoustic songs. Among the regulars at the bar were local jazz musicians Leroi Moore, who played a variety of horns, and drummer Carter Beauford. Sharing an interest in music—if not musical styles—Matthews invited them to contribute to his demos. The three started playing out together, adding high school bass prodigy Stefan Lessard to the mix. Boyd Tinsley came onboard after he added violin to one of Matthews's demos.

From the start the band was an eclectic mix. Part jam band, part acoustic balladeers, part jazzy rock ensemble, the band's resultant music was informed by multifarious styles. This included Matthews's interest in African music and the jazz and jam inclinations of the other musicians. Their harmonic hodgepodge took the form of a rock band, and the music they played was ultimately built on the core of Matthews's vocals and his percussive acoustic guitar playing.

The Dave Matthews Band played its first gig in April 1991 and set out on the college circuit. In a development that was equal parts Grateful Dead and R.E.M., dedicated fans began filling venues and demanding airplay. College radio stations started spinning the band's *Remember Two Things*, a self-released live album that eventually sold 150,000 copies. The impressive indie sales, combined with DMB's reputation as a solid concert draw, attracted major labels within the year. The band signed with RCA and released its major-label debut, *Under the Table and Dreaming*, in late 1994.

CHECKLIST ✓

Guitar . . . . Taylor 912ce, Gibson Chet Atkins SST, Martin HD-28

Setup . . . . Medium action

Strings . . . . D'Addario .011s

Pickups . . . . Fishman piezo

Amplification . . . Usually direct to PA

Effects . . . . Harmonizer

Tone . . . . Midrange "wonk," hint of overdrive, bright

Picking . . . . Flatpick

Attack . . . . Aggressive, funk-rock style

Signature traits . . . . Partial and open chords

Influences . . . . . . The Beatles, Adrian Belew, Robert Fripp

Overall approach . . . . Boisterous

SELECTED DISCOGRAPHY

Remember Two Things (RCA, 1993)
Under the Table and Dreaming
    (RCA, 1994)
Crash (RCA, 1996)
Live at Red Rocks 8.15.95
    (Bama Rags/RCA, 1997)
Before These Crowded Streets
    (RCA, 1998)
Live at Luther College (RCA, 1999)
Listener Supported (RCA, 1999)
Everyday (RCA, 2001)
Busted Stuff (RCA, 2002)
Live at Folsom Field, Boulder, Colorado
    (RCA, 2002)

RECOMMENDED CUTS

 "Ants Marching" (*Under the Table and
    Dreaming*)
"Crash into Me" (*Crash*)
"Let You Down" (*Crash*)
"Lie in Our Graves" (*Crash*)
"The Space Between" (*Everyday*)

Forgoing electric guitar and even guitar solos in order to keep the feel heavily acoustic, the arrangements were surprisingly complex for a pop album. The use of saxophone and violin would have been sneered at in almost any other band, especially one that had gained credibility as a jam band *à la* the Dead, Blues Traveler, and Phish. Matthews also had a proven ability to lend direction to rambling jams with catchy hooks and singable choruses.

The group followed up in 1996 with *Crash*, which debuted at No. 2 on the *Billboard* charts, establishing DMB as a commercial and critical success. "Crash into Me," "Let You Down," and "Lie in Our Graves" all spotlighted Matthews's quirky sense of rhythm and riffing. Running smack up against mainstream expectations, buyers flocked to songs with strange chords, weird beats, and very little rock guitar.

DMB had built its initial success on touring, and the band capitalized on its history by releasing several live albums (which also beat back the bootleggers). *Before These Crowded Streets*, released in April 1998, was a studio recording but revealed more live, improvisational spirit than any of the band's prior studio albums. Matthews then took time out to record an acoustic album with his guitar-playing partner, Tim Reynolds. Between sold-out tours, DMB recorded an album with producer Steve Lillywhite that was shelved after completion, reportedly due to friction with the producer over the dark tones he added to the band's sound (although Lillywhite had been responsible for distilling DMB's finest elements for *Under the Table and Dreaming*). DMB replaced that record in 2001 with the pop sheen of *Everyday*. In addition to the funky "I Did It," the album featured the melancholy "The Space Between," a lugubrious tune that stands on top of a two-chord acoustic figure. Curiously, its dark vibe recalls the sound of Peter Gabriel—when he was produced by Lillywhite.

Unable to stem the onslaught of bootleggers and Internet posters who had gotten their hands on the original Lillywhite sessions, DMB finally released that music as *Busted Stuff* in 2002. It showed a more mournful side of the band, which actually endeared them to those who had been put off by *Everyday*'s spit-and-polish sound.

DMB remains one of the world's top concert draws, and its love of eclecticism should keep the band in the musical mainstream for years to come.

GEAR & SETUP

For years Matthews used a black Gibson Chet Atkins SST almost exclusively, and the midrange-heavy tone he dialed up with this acoustic-electric (powered by Fishman piezo pickups) came to define his sound. Setting his action at a medium height makes for reasonable playability while allowing the snappy attacks that characterize his percussive style.

His main guitar in recent years has been a small-bodied Taylor 912ce. He has also relied on Martins, and his collection includes an HD-28 (with a Fishman Gold Plus Natural 2 pickup) and a D12-28 12-string. He played a Martin Vintage Series dreadnought on tour with Tim Reynolds (who used a Martin D-35). In 1999, Martin announced the limited-edition DM3MD signature model, which had a low-profile neck with a slight V shape.

His main guitar in recent years has been the Taylor 912ce, another small-bodied instrument. His other acoustics include a Lakewood M-32 (with AER pickup). All of Matthews's guitars are strung with D'Addarios (usually .011s), and he uses Jim Dunlop .60mm picks.

Matthews's acoustic is literally and figuratively the center of DMB's live show, and its output is the result of a complex though not heavily processed rig. Two Nady Wireless transmitters split his guitar signal, each feeding Meyer Sound EQs; their settings reflect a need for brightness and midrange to cut through the band's heavily layered sound. Both signals pass through an Eventide 3000 GTR Harmonizer before being split again: one signal goes straight to the PA, while the other is EQ'd and amped for onstage monitoring (with Meyer Sound USM-1 Stealth Monitors). When the band is taping live shows, which it frequently does, he also mics the guitars with a B&K 4051-A.

One secret to Matthews's unique acoustic timbre comes with significant help from his soundman. The guitar signal sent to the PA is also bussed to a Fender Hot Rod Deluxe amplifier, miked, and returned to be blended into the mix. With this clever routing, Matthews is able to add a bit of amp overdrive to the natural, clean signal coming off his guitar.

His signal chain has also included a White 5024 digital multi-effects processor, Meyer Sound S-1 processor (for clipping protection), Crest 7001 power amp, API 512 preamp, and Rocktron MIDI pedals.

STYLE & TECHNIQUE

Matthews's strumming is aggressive, and he plays the guitar almost as if it were an electric (contrast this approach with that of Peter Buck, who plays his electrics like acoustics). He wears his guitar high, eschewing rock-star cool for access to the neck.

Much of DMB's music is built on brief (two- or four-bar) cycling passages; from this foundation, the band's orchestration builds and the basis of extended jams is established. Matthews's hook-laden figures tend to incorporate a variety of elements at once. Arpeggios, glissandos, slapping, double-stops, and single-note lines might all be heard within a few contiguous instrumental phrases.

The mixed bag of techniques is further offset with Matthews's keen sense of syncopation. In this respect, his approach has much in common with classic funk, where bite-sized phrases lend momentum and groove with their off-kilter feel. Matthews has also stated he uses partial chords to capture a sound that he can't get with standard chords. Bearing in mind that his guitar is the only polyphonic instrument in the band (no second guitar, no keys), he obviously has enough confidence in DMB's musical bed to not add full-voiced chords. The style is consistent with the guitars in South African music, which Matthews may have drawn on from Paul Simon, Sting, or his own early years in Africa.

LESSON

Matthews is a master of the two-bar catch phrase. Within a very brief song introduction, often played by a lone acoustic, he establishes groove and a hook. The ideas often come in question-and-answer form. In **Ex. 1** there are two "questions" (bars 1 and 3) and a single answer (bars 2 and 4 are identical). There's a *lot* of technique and movement at work here, including hiccuping leaps, sliding double-stops, and bends. Matthews is also fond of using glissandos—quick slides up or down a string—within such parts. Though unpitched, they function as melody.

Ex. 1

Example 2 combines two elements heard on a number of DMB songs. Several of the band's tunes, notably riff-based rockers such as "Spellbound," revolve around stacked-5th chords. Power chords like these are ubiquitous in rock, but when parsed out note by note they reveal wide intervals that make for great funk riffs or sprawling arpeggios. Picked arpeggios are the game here, with another favorite Matthews move on top: using open upper strings as a pedal. As on a track like "Crash into Me," the pedals cut through with the help of doubled notes up top.

Ex. 2

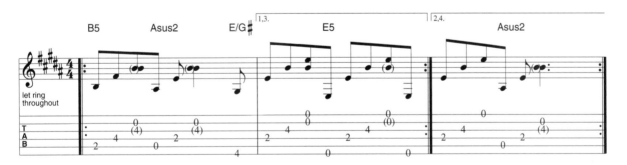

Folk and funk are unlikely bedfellows, but Matthews pairs the two for another catchy intro (**Ex. 3**). Capoing up at the 8th fret contributes a bright timbre as open (to the capo) strings ring against notes fretted as high as the 12th fret. Strum freely at first, and let the mild dissonance of the open 4th string against the sliding 6ths come out. But be ready to hone in for the second measure's figure, where 3rd-string hammers alternate with the open 1st string.

Ex. 3

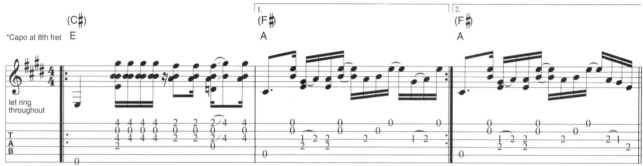

*All notes, chords, and tab numbers are notated relative to capo position; chord symbols in parentheses indicate actual key (C).

ON THE CD

Track 1: Tuning

Track 2: Neil Young Ex. 1

Track 3: Neil Young Ex. 2

Track 4: Neil Young Ex. 3

Track 5: George Harrison Ex. 1

Track 6: George Harrison Ex. 2

Track 7: George Harrison Ex. 3

Track 8: George Harrison Ex. 4

Track 9: Paul Simon Ex. 1

Track 10: Paul Simon Ex. 2

Track 11: Paul Simon Ex. 3

Track 12: Keith Richards Ex. 1

Track 13: Keith Richards Ex. 2

Track 14: Keith Richards Ex. 3

Track 15: James Taylor Ex. 1

Track 16: James Taylor Ex. 2

Track 17: James Taylor Ex. 3

Track 18: Pete Townshend Ex. 1

Track 19: Pete Townshend Ex. 2

Track 20: Pete Townshend Ex. 3

Track 21: Eagles Ex. 1

Track 22: Eagles Ex. 2

Track 23: Eagles Ex. 3

Track 24: Tom Petty Ex. 1

Track 25: Tom Petty Ex. 2

Track 26: Tom Petty Ex. 3

Track 27: Tom Petty Ex. 4

Track 28: Peter Buck Ex. 1

Track 29: Peter Buck Ex. 2

Track 30: Peter Buck Ex. 3

Track 31: Dave Matthews Ex. 1

Track 32: Dave Matthews Ex. 2

Track 33: Dave Matthews Ex. 3

All tracks performed by Rich Maloof and recorded at OopStudios in Brooklyn, New York.

ACKNOWLEDGMENTS

The authors wish to acknowledge the following for their help in creating this book:

Thanks to our editors at Backbeat Books—Richard Johnston, Nancy Tabor, and Amy Miller—for their ongoing interest and support in making *The Way They Play* books a reality. Additional thanks to Philip Chapnick, who encouraged us to find a home for this series within his publishing group.

Steve "Chinner" Winstead, guitar tech for Mike Campbell, called a band meeting to provide us with accurate information for the Tom Petty chapter. Thank you Chinner, Alan "Bugs" Weidel, Tom Petty, Mike Campbell, and Mary Klauzer of East End Management. From the R.E.M. camp, Peter Buck's guitar tech, DeWitt Burton, and Warner Bros.' Jim Baltutis provided invaluable just-in-time assistance.

Thanks to fellow guitar geek Pete Prown, who can hold five offspring and 50,000 *Greenscene* readers at bay to extol the virtues of sitka tops over spruce. His candid critiques are almost as welcome as his support. Look for Pete's books *Legends of Rock Guitar* (Hal Leonard, 1997) and *Gear Secrets of the Guitar Legends* (Backbeat Books).

HP Newquist would like to thank:

Thanks to Rich Maloof, who got more than he bargained for when he signed on to do another book with me. If this book is a good read and a smooth listen, then the credit is his. Masterful editor and accomplished guitarist, he put together the music and text like no one could have. I will always appreciate his friendship, hard work, and refrigerator stocked with beer—in that order. Rich, go take a vacation. You deserve it.

Thanks to Trini, Madeline, and Katherine, who have come to appreciate the sound of a beautiful 12 string, and now know the difference between a Les Paul and a Stratocaster. Every time I sit down with a guitar or a computer, it is for the three of them.

Finally, I've been lucky enough to have friends and family who have supported my guitar playing and book writing for many years. Thanks to my parents, brothers and sisters, friends, bandmates, and teachers—all of whom have put up with incredibly loud amplifiers and very late nights.

Rich Maloof would like to thank:

This series was dreamed up by Harvey Newquist, as was the idea to involve me. Thanks, Harvey, for the professional justification to play more guitar and hang out with you.

Thanks to Andrea Rotondo, Emile Menasché, Jesse Gress, T.J. Baden of Taylor Guitars, and Dick Boak of C.F. Martin & Co.

Thanks to Dr. Beau Breslin for his perennial encouragement in writing and playing. And thanks for talking me out of it when I wanted to quit the damn guitar in 1986.

My wife, Kris, gets special thanks for tolerating not only my guitar playing but me in general. Big thanks to son Daniel for the magic drool on my strings.

Thanks to my long-gone and still-missed grandparents, Tom and Rose Turck, for my first real acoustic.

PHOTO CREDITS

Jay Blakesberg: pages 15, 31, 45, 52, 66, 74, 84
© Larry Hulst / Michael Ochs Archives.com: page 23
Michael Ochs Archives.com: page 59
Neil Zlozower: page 38

ABOUT THE AUTHORS

HP Newquist and his writing have appeared in publications as diverse as *The New York Times, Rolling Stone, USA Today, Variety, Billboard*, and *Newsweek*. He has written more than a dozen books, including *The Way They Play: The Blues-Rock Masters* (with Rich Maloof, published by Backbeat Books), *Music & Technology* (Billboard Books), *The Yahoo! Ultimate Reference Guide to the Web* (Harper-Collins), *The Brain Makers* (Macmillan), and *Legends of Rock Guitar* (with Pete Prown, published by Hal Leonard). Newquist was editor-in-chief of *Guitar* magazine, and his other magazine work has covered topics from musicians and medicine on to artificial intelligence and virtual reality. He has several film credits, including the Emmy-nominated music documentary *Going Home* for the Disney Channel. He has been playing guitar since he was 15, which seems like a very long time ago.

Rich Maloof is an editor, writer, and musician based in Brooklyn, New York. He is the author of numerous instructional pieces for musicians, including the books *The Way They Play: The Blues-Rock Masters* (with HP Newquist, published by Backbeat) and *Joe Satriani: Riff by Riff* (Cherry Lane), and he is writing the forthcoming biography of legendary amplifier designer Jim Marshall for Backbeat. Maloof served as editor-in-chief of *Guitar* magazine until 1998, when he launched his own business directing content for books, magazines, and Web sites. Among his clients to date are Berklee Press, *Billboard*, CNN, the For Dummies series, TrueFire, and Yahoo! He has sustained his passionate though occasionally adversarial relationship with the guitar for over 25 years.

WHEN IT COMES TO MUSIC, WE WROTE THE BOOK.

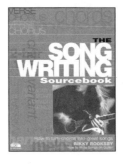

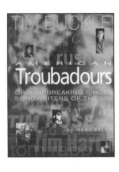
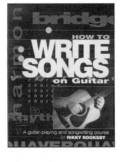